QUEENS

QUEENS
WOMEN IN POWER THROUGH HISTORY

PHYLLIS G. JESTICE

amber
BOOKS

First published in 2022

Published by
Amber Books Ltd
United House
North Road
London
N7 9DP
United Kingdom
www.amberbooks.co.uk
Instagram: amberbooksltd
Pinterest: amberbooksltd
Facebook: amberbooks
Twitter: @amberbooks

ISBN: 978-1-83886-227-5

Project Editor: Michael Spilling
Designer: Keren Harragan
Picture Research: Terry Forshaw

Printed in China

CONTENTS

INTRODUCTION

The *Mahābhārata*, one of the two great Sanskrit epic poems of ancient India, proclaims that countries ruled by a woman will sink like stone boats in a river. When created, this highly influential text both reflected the worldview of its authors and helped shape the notion through Indian history that rule is not safe in female hands. Such negative pronouncements about women exercising power have pervaded much of global history. For Chinese commentators through most of the imperial period, rule by women was considered unnatural and abhorrent to heaven. Similarly, the core texts of the Abrahamic religions emphasize that women should be subordinate to their husbands and that women's place is in the home – after all, they are daughters of Eve, who first caused the fall of humankind, and must pay the penalty eternally.

OPPOSITE: Hatshepsut, the fifth pharaoh of Egypt's Eighteenth Dynasty, took pains to associate herself with the male symbols of rule. Statues and reliefs depict her sometimes as female, sometimes as completely biologically male, and sometimes as a mixture of male and female. The latter is the case in this statue, now in New York's Metropolitan Museum of Art, which shows her in male garb but with the breasts of a woman, wearing the headdress that was typical of male rulers.

RIGHT: This medal was produced in 1887 to commemorate British Queen Victoria's 50th jubilee. It shows the monarch at ages 18 and 68. She reigned until her death in 1901.

OPPOSITE: In this portrait, now on display in the Great Hall at Hampton Court, Henry VIII chose to be painted with his son Edward and his third wife Jane Seymour, despite the fact that Jane had died shortly after Edward's birth.

Almost universally, commentators historically believed that women should not have power over states, since they will play favourites, squander resources and generally lack the courage necessary in a ruler. Many kingdoms through history have limited or outright forbidden female rule, at times see-sawing between acceptance and condemnation. For example, Sweden between 1593 and 1720 permitted female succession to the throne twice and banned it twice, only finally allowing it again in 1980. French Salic law denied the throne to women and had an impact on most of Europe for centuries. Such bans on female rule have been established as recently as the creation of the German Empire in 1871 and Japan's Meiji Restoration in 1889. In their effort to stress the impossibility of women's rule, the officials behind the Meiji reforms even declared the early Japanese empress Jinqu to have been a legendary rather than a historical figure. Yet Jinqu's official tomb can still be visited in Nara.

Women have ruled the kingdoms of the earth; we see them in the historical record as early as the third millennium BC. As with the Meiji declaration, at times there have been conscious efforts to erase these women from memory, to downplay their role or to vilify them. Sovereign women are a necessary by-product of hereditary monarchy: if royal authority is vested in a single lineage and no male is available to rule, royal blood trumps biological sex. In other words, it is preferable to have a queen than to look beyond the royal family for a king. Particularly in monogamous countries, rulers have decided as they aged that a girl was better than nothing, and bequeathed the throne to daughters or other female relatives. For example, between AD 300 and 1800, 30 women were queens regnant – sovereign rulers – over major European

BELOW: The legendary Empress Jinqu of Japan supposedly ruled in the third century AD. This woodblock print depicting her was created by Tsukioka Yoshitoshi in 1880.

states. They all had one crucial factor in common: they inherited because they did not have brothers, although in many cases their fathers tried desperately to beget a son. We need only think of the much-married Henry VIII of England, whose one longed-for son died young, to feel the weight of longing for a male heir. It is only in the twenty-first century that we have begun to see a breakdown of male-preferred primogeniture, with both Denmark and England passing laws mandating the accession of the ruler's eldest child, whether male or female.

QUEEN: A PROBLEMATIC TITLE

Even the use of the English word 'queen' to describe a female sovereign is confusing, since it comes from the Old English *cwen*, which simply means 'wife of a king.' For many, the term 'queen' still implies a member of the royal family in the passenger seat, rather than driving the state; historians have to add modifiers such as 'queen regnant' or 'queen consort' or 'queen mother' to differentiate them. Ruling women and their advisers have had to confront the expectations that their very title raises in many languages. Thus, in this book we will see women purposely crowned as 'king' rather than queen in the language of their land, in an effort to express the reality of their power and independent rule. Perhaps those female rulers were most fortunate who lived in lands with ungendered terms for a ruler, such as *pharaoh* in Egypt, *mepe* in Georgia or *ariki* for a Māori paramount chief.

Such gender neutrality in formal titles probably helped to some extent, but women still had to confront their subjects' assumption that the ruler would be biologically male. Some female rulers therefore found it expedient to actually present themselves to the world as male, from Hatshepsut of ancient Egypt to the nineteenth-century Lakshmi Bai of Jhansi. Nonetheless, sovereign women were probably ultimately most successful not by pretending they were male (at least in propaganda) as they were by proclaiming their own exceptionalism to the normal rules that governed their societies. Many female kings have claimed, as did Maria Theresa of Austria or Elizabeth I of England, that rulership transcends womanhood. Indeed, it is certainly no coincidence that the British legal doctrine of the king's two bodies first appeared in print in 1562, during Elizabeth's reign. This doctrine argues that a ruler has a 'body natural' – actual flesh and blood – but also a 'body politic,' the God-given rule that transcends the mere human body and the constraints of biological sex. The two merge as 'the crown,' which itself far exceeds gender expectations, or indeed human fallibility.

Although biological accident has led to the accession of queens regnant, the patriarchal nature of almost all societies in the past has complicated the ability

OPPOSITE: **In her 1970 tour of New Zealand, Queen Elizabeth II invested Māori Queen Te Arikinui Te Atairangikaahu as a Dame Commander of the British Empire. Although the Māori royal family does not play a political role, its rulers nevertheless exercise considerable influence.**

or even desire of these heiresses to actually rule. Most female sovereigns have accepted the dynastic imperative that put them on the throne in the first place – they have needed an heir. That has usually meant that they had to marry and if possible produce an heir, and then the ruler and her people have had to negotiate what it means for a queen to rule a country, but a husband to rule his wife. The five women who inherited the throne of Navarre between 1274 and 1555 all turned actual rule over to their husbands, in some cases despite the wishes of the Navarrese nobles, who were wary of foreign influence in their little country. Others, like Melisende of Jerusalem, had followers who resorted to force to assure that their husbands gave them at least some role in governance. From the sixteenth century onwards, a rising tide of nationalism served to limit the actual power of a 'prince consort,' but as we will see, even the twentieth century saw tensions over the notion of a husband being his own wife's subject. The only other option was not to marry at all, as was true of the Korean queens Seondeok, Jindeok and Jinseong, and, of course, the first Elizabeth of England.

Female sovereignty has been rare, but the nature of monarchy itself has given the women of royal families power, sometimes great power, over the destinies of their kingdoms. The word 'monarchy' itself – which means 'the rule of one' – is deeply misleading. Monarchy is a family affair. To some extent all rulers in world history have been co-rulers, sharing power with family members and favourites. The line between a ruler's household and the administration of a state has traditionally been blurred, especially before the rise of large professional bureaucracies. If the 'national' treasury is kept in a chest at the foot of the queen's bed, she naturally plays some role in its distribution. The very framing of a monarchy, with formal presentation and etiquette to underline the ruler's right to

BELOW: **Joanna (or Jeanne) I of Navarre unified her small country with France upon her marriage to King Philip IV; thanks to France introducing Salic law, the Navarrese regained independence under her granddaughter.**

13. JOHANNA KÖNIGIN VON NAVARRA,
1284 VERMÄHLT MIT KÖNIG PHILIPP IV. VON FRANKREICH.

LEFT: **This illustration depicts the marriage of Melisende, heiress of the Kingdom of Jerusalem, to Count Fulk of Anjou in 1129, from a deluxe manuscript of William of Tyre's *Chronicle* (c.1470).**

command, is a household matter in which the women of the royal house play a part. Wives, concubines, sisters, aunts and, above all, mothers of royal houses have all had essential functions in the world's monarchies.

THE ROLE OF QUEEN CONSORT

Often, a queen consort has played a complementary role to a king, for example, displaying kindness and generosity to temper the masculine sternness and firmness of their husbands. Queens consort have sometimes exercised great power, their husbands elevating their wives' importance to buttress the position of their heirs, or out of love or in recognition of their spouses' intelligence and abilities. At times, the power of the consort has left historical traces, as when queens are described as interceding to support a cause. In other cases, as in much of Chinese history, the influence of consorts is best described as 'shadow power,' whereby they have had to work within an intellectual framework that assumed women are inferior by nature. Some modern commentators have described a royal spouse's role as 'soft power' and characterized their purpose as influence rather than formal authority.

Royal spouses have often been strongest when either bureaucratic structures or their husbands have been weakest. The Mongol khans relied heavily on mothers and daughters as well as wives because they needed a person on the spot to serve as a viceroy. Other royal women have led troops in battle, guarded key fortresses (for example, Emma of France's defence of Laon) or raised reinforcements for their husbands. Royal wives have

ABOVE: **Although too many sons could create chaos, most kings were eager to produce male heirs. This manuscript account of Chinggis (Ghengis) Khan from c.1596 shows the great Mongol conqueror's ancestor Tumanba Khan with his wife and their nine sons.**

negotiated treaties, won concessions from enemies and performed many other tasks when their husbands needed somebody trustworthy who could wield the authority of the crown. They have also taken control of government as a whole when the male ruler has been absent or incapacitated.

Yet, however it has been defined, the influence or actual power of a consort has been conditional – derived from and granted by the husband. The derivative nature of the queen consort's power is apparent, for example, in Byzantine imperial ceremonies in which the patriarch crowns the emperor, but it is the emperor who confers the crown upon his wife. In ancient Rome, the title augusta had to be formally conferred by an emperor on his wife or the other female family member he wished to honour. While consorts have governed, led troops in battle and held the power of life and death, that power could be taken away from them. Throughout most of global history, a husband could dismiss a wife, strip her of wealth and authority and even order her execution. The only time such women have had any recourse is when the family of their birth was too prominent for the king to risk angering them. For example, it is argued that the German emperor Henry II did not divorce his barren wife Kunigunde only because her family was too powerful to slight. We can see the results of such a divorce when Sulayman of Mali repudiated his wife Kossi so that he could marry a commoner in c.1350 and Kossi led her family in an attempted coup. Although Sulayman's divorce provoked a minor civil war, the families of queens consort have rarely gone to such lengths to protect their daughters.

The political balance, however, could be sensitive, as rulers weighed the advantages and disadvantages of marrying elite women within their kingdom. Such a practice worked well in the kingdom of Biu (present-day Nigeria), where kings married multiple local women to link themselves to various clans. By contrast, emperors in the early Chinese dynasties usually found their mates from the families of high-ranking officials. By the Song Dynasty, however, the danger of those relatives-in-law cultivating their power even at the emperor's expense led emperors to prefer lower-class women, sometimes even commoners, as their mates. Perhaps the most extreme example of such a fear of encroaching relatives by marriage can be seen in the Ottoman Empire, where for over a century the sultans did not marry at all; instead, they fathered their children with slave concubines.

The habit in many cultures for kings to choose members of foreign royal houses as their consorts also created impediments, sometimes insurmountable, to a consort's exercise of power. A matter for concern was that the wife might be a foreign spy or perhaps would work to further the interests of her birth family, which was, of course, occasionally the case. More often, such a fear was probably based on rumour-mongering, but was still dangerous to the queen if the king came to believe the stories. Even when a new queen was not suspected of complicity with a foreign power, her very foreignness set her at a disadvantage. When a royal marriage was arranged, the girl was sometimes sent to her bridegroom's court to learn the language and customs; in other cases, she was thrust into a situation of bewildering strangeness, unable even to understand the language of her husband or many of her attendants. Such must have been the case for the 12-year-old Byzantine

BELOW: The tomb of the German imperial couple Henry II and Kunigunde, in Bamberg Cathedral, Germany, which they founded together in the early eleventh century. Both are canonized saints.

LEFT: **The wedding of Tsar Nicholas II and Alix of Hesse, who took the name Alexandra upon marriage. Laurits Tuxen painted the scene in 1895, shortly after the ceremony took place; it now hangs in the State Hermitage Museum, Saint Petersburg, Russia.**

OPPOSITE: **Catherine of Braganza (1638–1705) had the misfortune of being married to the womanizing Charles II of England; he fathered more illegitimate children than any other king of England, but Catherine herself was childless. Painting after Peter Lely, c.1665.**

Theophanu, sent west in the 970s to marry German emperor Otto II. She is not visible in political affairs for several years after their marriage, time she needed to learn the language and ways of her new lands. Several Ottoman sultanas, starting as foreign-born slaves, only became politically active after they had mastered Turkish. For some consorts, foreignness remained a grave stumbling block for their entire lives, as with the tsarina Alexandra, last empress of Russia, who never spoke the court language of French or Russian well, and who had a strong German accent until her death.

MONARCHY: KEEPING IT IN THE FAMILY

Some of the strongest queens consort have been closely related to their husbands; carrying a share of the dynasty's blood in their own veins lent them authority and tied them particularly closely to the interests of the royal house. A number of monarchies even had a tradition of brother-sister incest, among them not only the well-known case of Egypt, but Hawaii, Polynesia and several African royal families. Such marriages tended to reinforce the unique status of the royal house, but also gave women power in a way that their society found acceptable. In polygamous societies, such marriages could be perpetuated without serious risk of genetic defects, since the royal couple often had different mothers. Weakening the genetic pool was a danger, however, as can be seen in the progressive debility of the Habsburgs, who engaged in first-cousin and even uncle-niece marriages to preserve the tightly knit nature of their family 'firm.' Nonetheless, it is not a coincidence that a number of Habsburg women were trusted with great authority and that their lineage made their rule more acceptable.

BELOW: **Pharaoh Akhenaten of Eighteenth Dynasty Egypt (c.1345 BC) and Queen Nefertiti promoted the worship of a single god, Aton. Here, the god is portrayed as the sun disk, shedding his blessing on the royal couple and their three daughters (Neues Museum, Berlin).**

Unless she was an heiress, a queen's position very often depended on her stage in the life cycle. Young women usually counted for little except as diplomatic pawns (although the boys of royal houses were also often bartered away for diplomatic or political advantage). A bride could, of course, sometimes sway her husband with her physical attractions, but in polygamous societies she had to compete with others for the ruler's attention and esteem. Whether polygamous or monogamous, the situation changed after the queen bore a child, especially a son. Mothers of sons, even if they were slave concubines, had rights in Islamic law. Bearing a potential heir made a woman a force to be reckoned with, elevating her prestige

RIGHT: **A nineteenth-century portrayal of Charles II, complete with his beloved spaniels, chatting with the famous Nell Gwyn, a low-born actress who was one of his favourite mistresses.**

as well as giving her a means to assert herself since courtiers curried favour, eying her future influence. Even in the Christian world, where divorce has been frowned on and often outright forbidden, pregnancy and childbirth were almost always the only assured means for a queen to preserve her place, not even to speak of her ability to exert influence. In nearly all cases, when a royal couple was childless the queen was blamed as barren. It cannot have been easy to have been Catherine of Braganza, the childless wife of Charles II of England, consigned to powerlessness and faced with the humiliation of her husband's never-ending succession of mistresses. Only a rare woman such as the Byzantine Theodora, who enjoyed a unique partnership with her husband Justinian, could hope to wield power even though she was childless.

THE POWER OF MOTHERHOOD

The majority of powerful royal women in this book won their power through motherhood, whether real or fictive. Almost every kingdom in the world has recognized not only the right but the absolute duty of a mother to protect her child; in polygamous societies, that duty was extended to embrace the senior wife's care for her husband's children by other women if she did not bear

In nearly all cases, when a royal couple was childless the queen was blamed as barren. It cannot have been easy to have been Catherine of Braganza, the childless wife of Charles II of England, consigned to powerlessness and faced with the humiliation of her husband's never-ending succession of mistresses.

BELOW: The influence of Buddhism helped several Asian ruling women gain and hold power, including Wu Zetian, China's only empress regnant. This statue of Vairocana, the supreme divinity, is from Henan in Shaolin, China. It is one of the masterpieces of Wei Dynasty Buddhist art.

children herself. Polygamy, which was the rule rather than the exception in the global history of monarchy, actually served to take pressure off the official or senior wife to produce a child, since the succession could be assured by a woman too lowly in rank to challenge her power.

When a ruler died leaving a child to inherit, the queen mother frequently came into her own, despite existing cultural stereotypes that denigrated women's abilities. The general view was that a male regent might usurp the throne, but not a mother; such confidence was only proven to be mistaken a few times, such as when Wu Zetian of China deposed her son and claimed the throne herself. Even imperial China, where orthodox Confucian thought decreed women incapable of ruling, saw about 30 dowager empresses who served as regents for their sons or stepsons, whereas French Salic law made an exception to the general rule excluding women from power in the case of regents. The annals of world history are filled with such women, although their presence is sometimes disguised by the legal fiction that a ruler is of age upon accession, even if biologically still a child.

One of the greatest constants in human nature is respect and reverence for motherhood, and the respect owed to mothers, enforced by cultures throughout the world, repeatedly catapulted the mothers of adult rulers into political prominence as well as giving them the regency for children. After all, what decent son could refuse when his mother asks him to do something? The Virgin Mary's position at the pinnacle of Christian saints is based on the premise that when she asks her son Jesus for something, he will respond favourably. Public displays of deference to queen mothers were normal, from Solomon's respect for Bathsheba to the Mughal emperor Akbar, who is said to have denied his mother Hamideh Banu's requests only once in her life. Even when mother and adult son quarrelled, they were usually soon reconciled, as was the case with Melisende of Jerusalem after her son Baldwin III seized power. A rare king such as Louis XIII, who drove his mother Marie de' Medici into impoverished exile, would have been reviled as an unnatural son.

QUEEN MOTHERS

Nowhere was the position of 'queen mother' more institutionalized than in much of sub-Saharan Africa before the colonial era. The position of these women was sometimes explained by means of a constitutive event, as when Queen Idia of Benin in the sixteenth century used her magic powers to win victory for her son in battle during a succession struggle. Other societies practised – and to some extent still practise – a system of dual monarchy, such as the Asante of western Africa. In their case, the royal lineage passes through the female line. The senior woman of the lineage (often the new

king's biological mother but sometimes another woman of the family) has the right to name the king, and is then inaugurated jointly with him. While the two have normally assumed separate tasks, they were equally responsible for the well-being of their people. Even in regions without such a formal position, the queen mother has frequently played a key role as counsellor and mediator. It is noteworthy, however, that it was expected the queen mother remain chaste, because of the fear that if she took a lover or husband she would lose impartiality. Such a belief was not limited to Africa; as Alfonso X of Castile put it in the statutory code Siete Partidas, a mother should be regent for a minor on the throne – as long as she did not remarry.

We should not forget that many kings did not have living mothers, thanks to women's function as biological females. While a woman of a ruling dynasty did not normally have primary responsibility for rearing her children, she still had to face the risks of childbirth, often repeatedly as high infant mortality encouraged large families. Faustina the Younger, wife of Roman Emperor Marcus Aurelius, was by no means uncommon as a mother of 12 children. Whether a consort or a queen regnant, pregnancy and childbirth could sideline a woman for months, even if all went well. Women such as Queen Anne of England were permanently debilitated by multiple pregnancies, in her case making it impossible for the invalid queen to play an active political role, even if she had had the intelligence and education to do so.

ROYAL WOMEN OPERATING IN A MALE WORLD

Most queens in world history have lived and worked in political environments that have been almost exclusively male. Unlike their male counterparts, few women rulers have been educated for the work of government. As a result, when women – whether consorts, mothers or sovereigns – have held power, the male world in which they have been expected to operate has viewed them with suspicion and often hatred. These women have mostly existed in a different arena to the men they needed to command; while men who aspired to government have studied politics, war or classic wisdom literature, women of royal families, with some variation by region, have much more likely been taught music, embroidery or how to give sexual satisfaction to a man. Women have also traditionally been expected to adhere to a different moral standard, one that emphasizes kindness and

BELOW: Queen Anne of England, Scotland and Ireland was the last ruler of the Stuart Dynasty. Although depicted in this engraving of 1715 with her only child to survive infancy, Duke William of Gloucester did not live long enough to inherit the throne upon Anne's death in 1714.

ABOVE: **Catherine the Great of Russia enjoyed a long political and emotional relationship with her chief minister Grigory Potemkin. In the Sky Atlantic/ Home Box Office TV series** *Catherine the Great* **(2019), the parts were played by Helen Mirren and Jason Clarke.**

chastity, whereas male rulers have been valued for their firmness and have frequently been admired for their promiscuity.

Under such circumstances, it is not very surprising that women rulers have often been vilified or simply left out of the histories. Rather than admiring Wu Zetian, the one empress regnant in Chinese history, over generations, scholars transformed her into an oversexed monster, an aberration who should never have been able to lay claim to a position of power. Such vilification has tended to be far more personal than that faced by male rulers; it has amounted to attacks on them, rather than on their policies. Above all, gender stereotypes have been mistakenly regarded as fundamental, immutable differences between the biological sexes, including the all-too-common view that women are weak-willed and sexually insatiable. Although some women rulers have been admired, it has usually either been because they embody stereotypes of womanhood or they have behaved in a man-like fashion – like, but never quite managing to be truly male. Many ruling women have been forced to a life of celibacy after their husband's death because of the cultural assumption that any lover would exercise a harmful influence. Women, both regents and sovereigns, have also had to work harder than the men they have married or borne in order to be seen as fit to rule, including consciously sponsoring charity and culture – activities that can provide visibility and influence.

Has the study of ruling women come of age? Historians have made considerable progress in recent decades by recognizing the complexities of female rule in a male political world and learning to read sources against the grain in order to shed light on how many of these strong women operated skilfully in their environments. We still have a way to go, however. For example, modern accounts of the Ottoman Empire in the sixteenth and seventeenth centuries, a period notable for its strong queen mothers, are still inclined to regard the influence of the harem as an illegitimate usurpation of power, a sign of the growing debility of Ottoman society rather than an adaptation to exploit strengths. Female rulers are often described as ambitious rather than bold, as devious rather than diplomatically astute and as intriguers and meddlers, all characterizations that are destructive to the reality of women's lives in the world's monarchies. Even genealogies still often leave out the women of royal families, overlooking their genuine contributions. To some extent, we will never know these great women of history as well as we know their menfolk; the sources simply leave too many gaps. However, we can and will do better in giving the women rulers of history the recognition they deserve.

BELOW: A royal visit. When Queen Elizabeth II and Prince Philip visited Copenhagen in May 1979, the two hereditary monarchs Elizabeth and Queen Margrethe II of Denmark took centre stage, flanked by Philip and Prince Henrik.

POWERFUL WOMEN OF THE ANCIENT WORLD

Who was the Queen of Sheba? Her visit to Solomon appears in both Hebrew scriptures and the Qur'an, offering a glimpse of a powerful independent ruler of the tenth century BC. No husband is mentioned, which suggests she was sovereign rather than a consort; her power can be seen in her wealth and the Qur'an's mention of her 'mighty throne,' an attribute otherwise credited only to God. Yet this Queen of Sheba remains a mystery beyond these two brief passages, although modern scholars think she may have ruled in what is present-day Yemen. We do not even know her name, although later legend calls her either Balkis or Makeda. The stories indicate that women's rule in ancient times was possible, but only hints survive.

OPPOSITE: **The Queen of Sheba's visit to King Solomon has fascinated many Christian artists for many centuries. This miniature by Hans Memling depicts the scene as it was imagined in the fifteenth century.**

RIGHT: **Aelia Flaccilla, wife of Theodosius the Great, was Roman empress 378–86. Famous for her charitable activities and defence of Christianity, she is recognized as a saint of the Orthodox Church. This bust, believed to represent her, is in the Metropolitan Museum of Art, New York.**

Other powerful ancient women seem more reliably documented in written sources, but on close examination the evidence often melts away. A good example is Esther, the Jewish saviour of her people during the Babylonian captivity. The biblical book of Esther tells a story rich with detail – how Esther was chosen to marry Ahasuerus (Xerxes) in a bride show, won his favour and interceded with her husband at a key moment, exhibiting great personal bravery. However, modern scholars consider the account largely legendary, invented after the fact to explain the festival of Purim.

Other women who appear in ancient literary sources have fallen victim to authors' lurid imaginations to the point that what they really did in life has been lost. A striking case is the legend of Semiramis. Her tales are probably based on a historic core; a woman named Shammuramat was regent in the Neo-Assyrian Empire at the end of the ninth century BC. Greek authors erected an enormous edifice upon that shallow foundation. They told that

RIGHT: Esther, looking apprehensive but resolute, is being prepared to appear before King Ahasuerus in this painting by Edwin Long (1878).

when her son came of age but was killed in battle, Semiramis disguised herself as her own child and ruled for 42 years, conquering much of Asia in the process. Such stories probably belong in the same category as Greek fantasies of a race of warrior women, the Amazons.

WOMEN IN ANCIENT GREECE

Classical Greek attitudes about women shaped many of their accounts of female rule, making it necessary to interpret such stories with caution. Herodotus, the 'father of history', discusses a number of influential women, but usually represents their roles negatively, apparently shocked that the women of Achaemenid-dynasty Persia played a political role. He tells, for instance, that the Persian Atosa (c.550–475 BC), daughter of Cyrus the Great and wife of Darius I, was 'powerful.' He credits her with ensuring the succession of her own son Xerxes rather than Darius' eldest son, and even claims that Atosa persuaded Darius to invade Greece because she wanted foreign slaves. The simple truth is that Darius I had ample reason to launch his invasion of Greece in 490 BC without being prompted by anyone, and Atosa's own son – with the blood of Cyrus and born after Darius became king – surely had a superior claim to the throne. Nonetheless, Herodotus' reports of 'meddling' Achaemenid women reveals his recognition of a fundamental truth, that monarchy is a family affair. Wives had access to husbands, and husbands could

ABOVE: **The legendary Queen Semiramis receives word of an uprising in Babylon in this 1669 painting by Adriaen Backer. As is typical of early modern European art, Backer has depicted the Middle Eastern queen as a northern European woman.**

(usually) trust their wives to act in the interests of the family. Lineage also mattered – a daughter of Cyrus the Great had status that could not be ignored, even if the culture in which she lived regarded her as 'only' a woman.

There is very little trustworthy contemporary evidence about female sovereigns or influential consorts before the Common Era. Sometimes we have only a name, such as Iskallata, apparently an Arab woman ruling in Syria, captured by the Assyrian Sennacherib I early in the seventh century BC. The earliest known monarch of Cambodia was Queen Soma in the first century CE, but again, we know little beyond her name. Archaeology helps, although interpretation is difficult without written accounts. Queen Pu-abi of Ur, for example, was clearly important. She was buried in c.2500 BC wearing a headdress of gold and lapis lazuli, with a gold cup in her hand. Even more significantly, she was interred with human sacrifices, probably because she was regarded as the representative of a god on earth. More than two and a half millennia later, human sacrifice also attended the burial of the first known ruler of Japan, a woman named Pimiku; over a hundred of her servants were buried alive around her tomb. For Pimiku, later written sources help in interpretation.

We are on slightly firmer ground with early Egyptian royal women. Meretneith (b. c.3000 BC) was possibly a sovereign ruler in the First Dynasty, although she may have been regent for her young son. She appears as 'king's mother' on a list of king's names, and her appearance there at all suggests power. Meretneith was also the only royal female of the dynasty to have great monuments at both Sakkara and Abydos, as was typical of kings. Her tomb was situated next to her husband's, with an enclosure for rituals, again as with the funerary practices for kings.

BY RIGHT OF INHERITANCE

Meretneith, like many Egyptian royal women, was probably her royal husband's sister or half-sister. Such 'adelphic' (brother-sister) marriages, known in Egypt and several other global monarchies, assured that the sacred blood of the royal house would not be diluted. Women who shared sacred blood of the pharaohs enjoyed a superior status that would have eased the transition to sole power – if the conditions were right. Above all, the precondition for almost all women with sovereignty in the ancient world and later was that no adult male of

BELOW: The crown of Queen Pu-abi, which was discovered in the royal tombs of Ur in Mesopotamia. Interlocking gold leaf wreaths, with lapis lazuli and carnelian beads and gold hair ribbons make this elaborate headdress weigh over 2.7 kg (6 lb). Pu-abi lived in c.2500 BC; she was about 40 years old when she died.

Nitocris is a shadowy figure, who seems to have taken the throne when there was no natural male successor to Pepi II.

the royal bloodline was available to ascend the throne. Meroitic Kush may have been matriarchal from the late second century BC until the early fourth century AD; at least, we know of nine ruling queens from their tombs in Meroë, a port city on the Nile. However, they were an exception.

Most of the ancient sovereign females we know about were Egyptians, their path to rule certainly enabled by their royal blood. Nitocris, who ruled in the First Intermediate Period (c.2150 BC) is a shadowy figure, who seems to have taken the throne when there was no natural male successor to Pepi II; we don't know her relationship to Pepi.

The first clearly attested Egyptian female pharaoh is Neferusobek (c.1760-c.1756 BC), who ruled for nearly four years at the end of the Twelfth Dynasty. She was probably Amenemhat IV's sister, and succeeded to the throne when he died childless. She ruled as king (pharaoh), the first royal woman in Egypt to be named as the female embodiment of the god Horus. Neferusobek appears in art bearing the regalia of male rule, but with a female body. That she was the last ruler of a dynasty suggests that crowning a woman might have been a desperate measure to stave off chaos. The same can probably be said of Tausret, the last pharaoh of the Nineteenth Dynasty (r. c.1198–c.1190 BC). A royal daughter and wife, Tausret first served as regent for her dead husband's son by another wife, but when the child died, she assumed the throne herself for lack of a male heir. We do not know if she died of natural causes or was overthrown, but her dynasty died with her.

BELOW: **Hatshepsut had herself portrayed in art with the attributes of a male pharaoh and sometimes even as an anatomical man, as in this statue, which includes the false beard that male rulers wore as a symbol of authority.**

Far more famous, largely because of the art she commissioned, is Egypt's next female pharaoh, Hatshepsut (r. c.1479–c.1458 BC). Like Neferusobek and Tausret, Hatshepsut was the daughter and wife of pharaohs. When her husband-brother Thutmose II died, Hatshepsut initially ruled as regent – 'Mistress of the Two Lands' – for the young son of a secondary wife. However, in the seventh year of her regency, Hatshepsut became pharaoh in her own name, assuming 'the five names' of pharaonic ritual and taking her place as the force to assure right order (*ma'at*) in the world. Why we do not know, although the primary role of pharaohs as intermediary between the gods and humankind suggests some sort of crisis for which a mere regent, not invested with full office, was inadequate. Step by step, Hatshepsut took on not just the titles but the ritual appearance of monarchy, to the point that in the art of her later reign she is depicted as a biological male.

There is no evidence that anyone ever tried to remove Hatshepsut from power during her 20-year reign, including her stepson Thutmose III, whom she raised well. In fact, Hatshepsut was a daughter of Thutmose I and his chief wife Ahmose, so in fact she had more royal blood in her veins than did the boy she displaced. She also assured her standing with the gods by obtaining an oracle from the god Amun, confirming her as the god's daughter and declaring her to be pharaoh. The impressive temples she had constructed in every major Egyptian city, the obelisks she commissioned (including the largest ever made in antiquity) and her own great mortuary temple at Deir el-Bahri all reinforced the authority she claimed as her birthright. Hatshepsut was successful and left Egypt prosperous and peaceful at the time of her death. Towards the end of his own 30-year reign, Thutmose III tried to erase Hatshepsut's memory by destroying evidence of her existence. The inconsistency of that destruction and its late date suggests to modern scholars that Thutmose was suffering a fit of jealousy because he could not live up to Hatshepsut's success, rather than deep resentment at having been kept from the throne in the first place.

FEMALE RULERS OF HALIKARNASSOS

The few other sovereign women of antiquity about whom we have information were also scions of the dynasties they came to rule. Closest to the Egyptian model are three women who ruled Halikarnassos in Asia Minor – Artemisia I in the late sixth and early fifth century BC, and Artemisia II and Ada in the fourth century. They rose to sovereignty despite Halikarnassos' Greek culture because the

ABOVE: **The mortuary temple of Hatshepsut at Deir el-Bahari is one of the greatest achievements of ancient Egyptian architecture. Constructed between the seventh and twentieth years of Hatshepsut's reign, plans for this great terraced edifice were repeatedly modified during construction.**

royal family practised adelphic marriage; all three had been married to their brothers and to some extent shared rule with them.

Artemisia I is the most famous since, as we will see, she personally led a small fleet during Xerxes' invasion of Greece in 480 BC. While we do not know the first Artemisia's position during her husband's lifetime, Artemisia II was co-ruler with her husband Maussollos. They worked together on a massive urban restructuring of Halikarnassos and planned the great dynastic memorial known as the Maussolleion. When Maussollos died, the Persian king simply let Artemisia II continue to act as satrap (although probably without the title), and she reigned peacefully until her death two years later. Similarly, Ada of Halikarnassos served as satrap after her husband died, and when Alexander the Great claimed the region, he formally appointed her to the office. She served him loyally, weeding out the last Persian resistance in the area.

In the wake of Alexander's conquests, a series of Hellenistic monarchies were established, and as usual with monarchies, women of the family played a role. When the lack of an adult male led these women to public power, they sometimes came to sticky ends, perhaps reflecting Greek cultural values. The fate of Deidania II (r. 235–231 BC) is an object lesson. She was the daughter of Pyrrhus II of Epirus, the last member of the Aeacid dynasty after her father and uncle died. Her rule, however, was not a success and her own nobles plotted to overthrow her. She was forced to take refuge in a temple, where her enemies murdered her. Another murder victim was Berenice III of Egypt, who became sole ruler in 81 BC. The Roman dictator Sulla arranged Berenice's marriage to her cousin Ptolemy X Alexander, intending that they should rule

together. When Berenice refused the match, the disgruntled cousin had her assassinated. However, at least Berenice was revenged; the populace rioted in outrage at the news of their queen's death and killed her would-be husband. She was more fortunate than Berenice IV. When King Ptolemy XII Auletes went to Rome, he left his daughter Berenice as regent. She, perhaps thinking he was never coming home, had herself proclaimed queen and ruled alone for three years. When her angry father returned, he defeated and executed the young woman in 55 BC. Perhaps the Ptolemaic Cleopatra VII (r. 51–30 BC) survived on the throne as long as she did because she always maintained the pretence of co-rule rather than sovereignty – with her brothers Ptolemy XIII and Ptolemy XIV, and then with Caesarion, her son by Julius Caesar.

Among women who held sovereign power simply because no male was available, the tale of Salome Alexandra (141–67 BC) makes a refreshing change. Salome Alexandra, of Judea's Hasmonean dynasty, married two successive kings of Judea. When the second died in 76 BC, he bequeathed the throne to his wife, rather than to one of his adult sons. We do not know the reason for his decision, but it was not unheard of in the region; John Hyrkanos had done the same on his death in 104 BC, although his eldest son immediately rebelled and seized the throne. In the case of Salome, there is no reason to suppose that the sons were incompetent; one had already held military commands, and, once she was established as queen, the mother appointed another as high priest, since as a woman she could not hold the office.

When King Ptolemy XII Auletes went to Rome he left his daughter Berenice as regent. She, perhaps thinking he was never coming home, had herself proclaimed queen and ruled alone for three years.

THE PROBLEMS OF A GREEK MOTHER

Olympias (b. c.375 BC), mother of Alexander the Great, is one of the most notorious women of ancient Greece. Her stormy relationship with her husband Philip II of Macedon may have led her to join the conspiracy that assassinated him in 336 BC. When Alexander set out to conquer the Persian Empire, Olympias engaged in a long power struggle with Antipater, the appointed regent of Macedon, clearly thinking she was the more appropriate person to rule for her absent son.

After Alexander died in 323 BC, Olympias vigorously defended the rights of her infant grandson to rule Macedon. In so doing, she personally led an army against another member of the royal family, Eurydike, who wanted to make her own husband king. The battle never took place since Eurydike's soldiers refused to fight Alexander's mother. Although successful in that encounter, the young king's position was insecure and Olympias still lacked formal authority. Denied official status, Olympias reportedly engaged in a campaign of terror, capturing and murdering enemies by any means available. After a long, confused power struggle, the queen mother was finally killed in 316 BC, as was the grandson she had tried so desperately to protect.

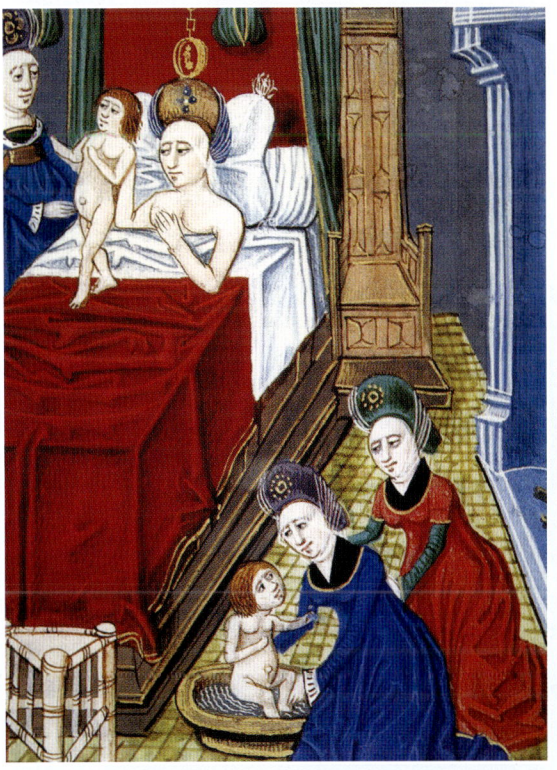

LEFT: This fifteenth-century miniature depicts Queen Olympias giving birth to Alexander, whose ability to stand and walk immediately is a portent of his extraordinary career.

Salome Alexandra ruled astutely until her death nine years later, reconciling the monarchy with the Pharisee sect and keeping the peace in that volatile region; her son the high priest succeeded.

PARTNERS IN RULE

Much more common than sovereign women in antiquity is evidence that royal women shared royal duties with their husbands. Sometimes such evidence is material. For example, Queen Puduhepa, wife of the Hittite king Hattusilis III (fl. c.1250 BC) played a public role. We know this because she had her own seal and used it on the king's foreign correspondence. This rare proof of shared rule carried on into the reign of their son, as Puduhepa continued to appear in royal correspondence. This has been interpreted as evidence that the son was weak, a typical example of the bias that still permeates many discussions of ruling women in history. In the case of Puduhepa, we can only guess why she was involved in government; the reason may have been as straightforward as husband and son recognizing her intelligence and political astuteness.

China is well known for Confucian-inspired beliefs that women are incapable of rule, but on closer examination the historical evidence is much more nuanced. Confucius was himself ambivalent on the subject of female rulers. During his own lifetime in the fifth century BC, the ruler of the kingdom of Wei withdrew from government, investing his wife, Lady Nanzi, formally with the tasks of government. Confucius praised her wisdom.

More customary than turning power over to one's wife was sharing the tasks of government. The king's wife enjoyed close proximity to the king. She could interact regularly with him, unconstrained by the formal etiquette that surrounds rulers in public. She could usually be trusted to act in the king's interest, because her fate was inextricably tied to that of her husband and their children. In new dynasties or kingdoms, sometimes the queen was the only person a king could trust and he would delegate important tasks or even control of the kingdom as a whole to her. If the queen was of royal blood, she was likely to have been raised in a politically charged environment and to have created a network of contacts and loyal supporters who could ease the tasks of rule.

While most royal marriages have been diplomatic affairs intended to gain alliances or influence, we should not rule out the possibility that husbands also listened to wives because they loved and esteemed them. Kings occasionally made love matches, and in such cases the queen often enjoyed great influence if not actual co-rule. Such was true of Berenice I, the second wife of Ptolemy I of Egypt. Berenice started her career at court as a lady-in-waiting to Ptolemy's first queen, but by 287 BC Ptolemy had renounced Queen Eurydice and married Berenice, although

BELOW: **Naptera, the wife of Egyptian pharaoh Ramesses II, sent this letter of friendship fo the Hittite queen Puduhepa in the thirteenth century BC. It has survived because the Akkadian text was incised into clay and the clay was then baked hard.**

the decision cost him the important family connections Eurydice had brought to the marriage. Berenice's influence led Ptolemy to renounce his children by his first marriage in favour of her own.

A number of Ptolemaic royal women did not rule but had a real impact on Egypt. Berenice II, who married her cousin Ptolemy III, for example, was especially noted as a literary patron – suggesting that she was mistress of considerable resources. Yet another Ptolemaic female, Arsinoë III (the wife of Ptolemy IV), played a visibly active role in politics. She urged on Egyptian troops in the Battle of Raphia, a task normally associated with a male ruler. Her political significance won international recognition as well. Several cities honoured her with statues, and when Rome sent Ptolemy IV a gift of purple clothing, Arsinoë also received special garb. Perhaps the ultimate sign of Arsinoë's political prominence was her demise; she was murdered in 204 BC at about the same time as the king, a backhanded accolade for someone too influential to leave alive.

ROMAN EMPRESSES

With the coming of Rome's imperial age, the same factors that caused rulers in other lands to look to their wives for support influenced Roman emperors, although the shadow of republican forms as well as notions of proper conduct for Roman matrons kept the empresses in the background for a considerable time. Behind the scenes, however, their influence and real power could be great. The precedent was established with Empress Livia (27 BC–AD 14), Augustus Caesar's wife and partner in the massive task of restoring Roman peace and prosperity. During his long reign, Augustus travelled through the empire frequently, leaving him dependent on eyes and ears in Rome. Livia's correspondence with Augustus was voluminous and her influence upon him decisive, for example, in arranging the marriage of Augustus' daughter Julia to her own son and eventually the succession of her son Tiberius as emperor. Livia's sway is the more striking because she bore no children to Augustus. She creates the impression of a strong-willed, intelligent woman who laboured indefatigably for the good of her family and empire. Through their long career, Livia also provided a model of matronly

modesty, highlighting a planned return to traditional morals. We can best see how important Livia was, however, in the honours the Senate awarded her after Augustus' death in AD 14, naming her augusta and making her chief priestess of the cult of her deified husband, complete with a lictor to march before her and demonstrate her status to the world. Soon after, empresses had real political power, for example, Agrippina the Younger, who reportedly dominated her husband Claudius.

Becoming a Roman emperor was risky, and short-lived dynasties and military usurpations do not typically allow strong roles for female family members. By the fourth century, however, the principle of hereditary succession was firmly established, and emperors from Theodosius I onwards adopted a conscious policy of elevating their wives' position to reinforce the dynasty. We see this with Flaccilla, Theodosius I's empress (d. AD 387). We know little of her day-to-day involvement in governance, however, her depiction on coinage in the full regalia of emperor proclaimed to the world that she was important.

RIGHT: **Livia Augusta was deified after her death. In this life-size marble statue from the mid-first century AD, she is depicted as the goddess Ceres, bearing sheaves of wheat and a cornucopia. The figure is modestly clad, portraying an ideal Roman matron of the early empire.**

Modern historians consider Flacilla's daughter-in-law Eudoxia as the de facto ruler of the eastern empire and demonstrates the value of women in positions of great authority when the legally rightful ruler, her husband Arcadius, was weak. Nonetheless, Eudoxia was only able to exercise power through Arcadius, rather than in her own right. Contemporaries report that she used their children to manipulate Arcadius into doing what she wanted, and that when people asked Eudoxia for help she would win the emperor's agreement by 'nagging.'

As Roman historians' characterization of Eudoxia as a 'nagger' suggests, males (whether great nobles, administrators or simply bystanders) have often resented the influence of queens. Their criticism was usually muted – as long as the queen enjoyed the ruler's favour. The high birth status of queens also usually afforded them protection. When a low-born woman married royalty, however, complaints about her influence could turn deadly. Such a situation did not normally arise in ancient Greece or Rome, but polygamous royal courts such as that of China allowed greater possibilities for a commoner to rise to real power, and for that power to backfire. Later rulers, both emperors and empresses, did well to consider the object lesson of Wei Zifu, a Chinese singing girl who became imperial favourite and in 128 BC was elevated to the rank of empress. Wei Zifu persuaded the emperor to name her son as heir, but a rival court faction exacted revenge, claiming that the empress' power over her husband was only secured by black magic. The emperor eventually believed her detractors, and both Wei Zifu and her son were driven to suicide.

ABOVE: Agrippina the Younger crowning her son, the emperor Nero. Note that, like the statue of Livia on the facing page, the figure of Agrippina carries a cornucopia, symbol of fertility and, in this case, motherhood.

MOTHER POWER: THE CASE OF REGENCY

Some peoples have allowed succession by any male adult blood relative to ensure that there be an able war leader. Most monarchies in history, however, have preferred direct father-to-son succession, so inevitably children at times ascended the throne, as fathers died young of disease or in battle, or simply failed to beget surviving offspring until late in life. When a child sits

WARRIOR QUEENS

ABOVE: 'The Battle of Salamis' by Wilhelm von Kaulbach (1868). Although the gods fly in to support the Greeks in this battle scene, Kaulbach chose to highlight the heroic Queen Artemisia.

Much of the opposition to female rule has been that women cannot fight. Yet, while most women are physically weaker than men, leadership of armies depends more on intelligence, organization and command than physically leading charges. When necessary, ancient queens proved they could provide that leadership. China recognized the role of Lady Hao, a queen of the Shang Dynasty (c.1200 BC) as a powerful military leader. Tomyris, queen of the Massagetae, defeated and killed Cyrus the Great of Persia (c.530 BC). Artemisia I of Halikarnassos commanded a squadron of the Persian fleet in the Battle of Salamis (480 BC) and did much better both in the engagement and in the counsel she gave Xerxes than most of his male commanders. Empress Jingo-kogu of Japan completed her husband's conquest of Korea after his death (c.AD 200), despite being pregnant while leading the campaign. The list could easily be extended.

The most impressive female generals of antiquity rose to prominence through rebellion. Vietnam owes its start as an independent state to Trung Nhi and Trung Trac. Their rebellion began c.AD 39 when a Chinese commander murdered Trung Trac's husband and raped her. The sisters organized a guerrilla movement to drive the Chinese out, then ruled jointly as queens.

ABOVE: **Two Vietnamese women on elephants represent the Trung Sisters in the annual Hai Ba Trung Parade in Saigon (26 April 1957).**

ABOVE: **Queen Zenobia of Palmyra, shown here bound in golden chains, looking her last upon her city. Painting by Herbert Schmalz (1888).**

The story of Boudicca (d. c.AD 60) also begins with rape and outrage, although she was already queen of the Iceni in Britain when this occurred. When Boudicca's husband died, the Roman governor seized the kingdom; when Boudicca protested, she was flogged and her two daughters were raped. Boudicca rallied the Iceni and their allies in a bloody rebellion, personally commanding her forces in battle. After several victories, Boudicca's army suffered defeat, and she took poison to avoid capture.

Most successful in her rebellion against Rome was Zenobia of Palmyra (d. c.AD 274) in present-day Syria. Ruling officially for her son, Zenobia took advantage of the disarray caused by repeated Roman defeats and internal power struggles. She declared herself free of Rome and an independent empress; the conquests led by her loyal general Zabdas gained most of Egypt and Syria, extending as far north as the Black Sea. Zenobia took personal command when the Romans regrouped and fought her way to defeat in AD 272. Although she was duly stripped of her kingdom and paraded in a Roman triumph, Zenobia lived on in Italy, in time marrying a Roman senator.

The Han Dynasty of China produced six empresses who held power as regents.

on the throne of a personal monarchy (in which the ruler is accountable for the tasks of governing), obviously somebody has to rule for him. But who? Male members of the royal family might try to seize power for themselves; favouring one noble faction would inevitably cause tension with other noble lineages, not to mention the chance of usurpation. Mothers were the safest option. It is universally assumed that a mother will love and nurture her child, acting in the child's best interests during a minority. Thus a child coming to the throne offered unique possibilities for women – queen mothers – to hold nearly unlimited power. Most women rulers we know of from the ancient world were regents after their husband's death. Some gracefully receded into retirement when the king reached adulthood; others, once they had experienced real power, were unwilling to relinquish it.

The Han Dynasty of China produced no fewer than six empresses who held power as regents. They were not formally invested as official rulers; the fiction was maintained, as it was later in Europe, that the emperor was actually doing the ruling, even as a young child. Court chroniclers of the Han instead invented a description for empress-regents that signalled the reality of their power – that the women would 'appear in court and pronounce decrees.' Several of these women perpetuated their influence by ensuring that young children ascended the throne. Thus, of the 12 emperors of the Eastern Han, eight came to the throne between the ages of three months and 15 years. Empress Liang, one of the most redoubtable regents, controlled the government for three different emperors in the period AD 144–159.

Further west, in the cut-throat Hellenistic courts, the accession of minors was rare and boy-kings such as Alexander the Great's own son were unlikely

RIGHT: **Cleopatra I of Egypt, depicted on this coin of Ptolemy VIII Euergetes as the goddess Isis (c.140 BC).**

REGENTS AND THEIR FAMILIES

The first empress regent of the Han was Lü (241–180 BC), wife of the first emperor of the dynasty, Liu Bang. When Liu Bang died, Lü ruled for her son; she had the rival son killed and tortured his concubine mother to death. Her regency caused tensions because she was the daughter of a powerful noble clan, and favoured her own kinsmen in government offices, replacing (even killing) her husband's relatives with her own. That might have been tolerable if her son had in due course taken up the reins of government and restored balance. However, Lü's eldest son died and she replaced him with another boy, guaranteeing that she remained in power. When the second youth became restive under her control, the dowager empress imprisoned him and appointed a third. Finally, her husband's relatives killed Lü in 180 BC and massacred her entire clan.

ABOVE: Xiwangmu, the Queen Mother of the West. Believed to rule the land of the immortals, Xiwangmu was often depicted in the funerary art of the Han Dynasty, as in this relief from the second century.

China's emphasis on filial piety meant that a daughter who became empress would naturally advance her kinsmen, causing tension, although not often to such a violent degree. In AD 222, Empress Lü's family was formally barred from government offices specifically to prevent such favouritism; in 422, female regency was forbidden (although it still happened occasionally). On the positive side of filial piety, Empress Dowager Dou ruled for her son long after he reached adulthood. He finally claimed power in AD 92, whereupon he killed his uncles and many of their supporters – but he refused to harm his mother.

to survive. In such an environment, women could rarely hold on to a regency or protect their children. An exception is Cleopatra I of Egypt (d. c.173 BC). Cleopatra was a daughter of Antiochus III of the Seleucid Empire, who arranged her diplomatic marriage to Ptolemy V of Egypt. Her birth status and enormous dowry assured the queen an important position that served as a prototype for later Ptolemaic royal women. Cleopatra's son Ptolemy VI inherited when he was only five years old, but Cleopatra was able to keep him safe and establish herself as regent. She governed Egypt well until her son matured. Although she always ruled for her son rather than as sovereign, Cleopatra I issued coins in her own name, an important marker of public authority. That this queen did well by the son in her care can be seen in his nickname – Philomater – a person who loves his mother.

Cleopatra's birth rank helped her gain and hold power, which was also a factor with the Roman regent Galla Placidia (b. c.AD 388). Her extraordinary career provided other advantages as well. A daughter of Emperor Theodosius I, Galla Placidia was in Rome when the Visigoths sacked the city in 410; she was captured and soon married the Visigothic king Ataulf. After his death, she returned to the empire to play a political role, keeping her loyal Gothic guards and using them against her feckless brother Emperor Honorius. Galla Placidia lost that fight and was exiled, but in 425 she returned to serve as regent for her minor son Valentinian III. Galla Placidia's prestige as a member of the

BELOW: **The Mausoleum of Galla Placidia in Ravenna, which was the capital of the Western Roman Empire during the regent's lifetime.**

Theodosian dynasty served her well among both Romans and barbarians (non-Romans), and the understanding she had gained of the Germans overrunning Roman territory enabled her in 435 to negotiate a treaty with the Vandals.

Except in extraordinary circumstances, the most powerful woman at an adult king's court was not his wife but his mother. Mothers were experienced and often controlled networks of power. Sometimes they had helped place a son on the throne or preserved it for him while he grew up. They had played a role in the king's education, and sons remembered the honour due their mothers, honour that frequently translated into influence. There is a striking example in Hebrew scripture's I Kings, which tells that the queen mother Bathsheba's stepson came to her, asking her to intercede with her own son Solomon on his behalf. When she appeared at court, Solomon rose to meet his mother, bowed to her and sat her on a throne at his right hand. Admittedly, in this instance the request failed, but the public nature of the respect Bathsheba received suggests she did better on other occasions, as when she convinced her husband King David to name her son as heir. A woman need not have even have been queen to wield influence as a king's mother. Helena, who started her career as a tavern servant and eventually became a Roman general's mistress, was her son Constantine's adviser when he won control of the empire. Constantine named Helena augusta, and she is credited with encouraging his support of Christianity.

BELOW: **The power of women's persuasion. In this 1646 painting by Gerbrand van den Eeckhout, Bathsheba wins King David's promise that Solomon will be his successor.**

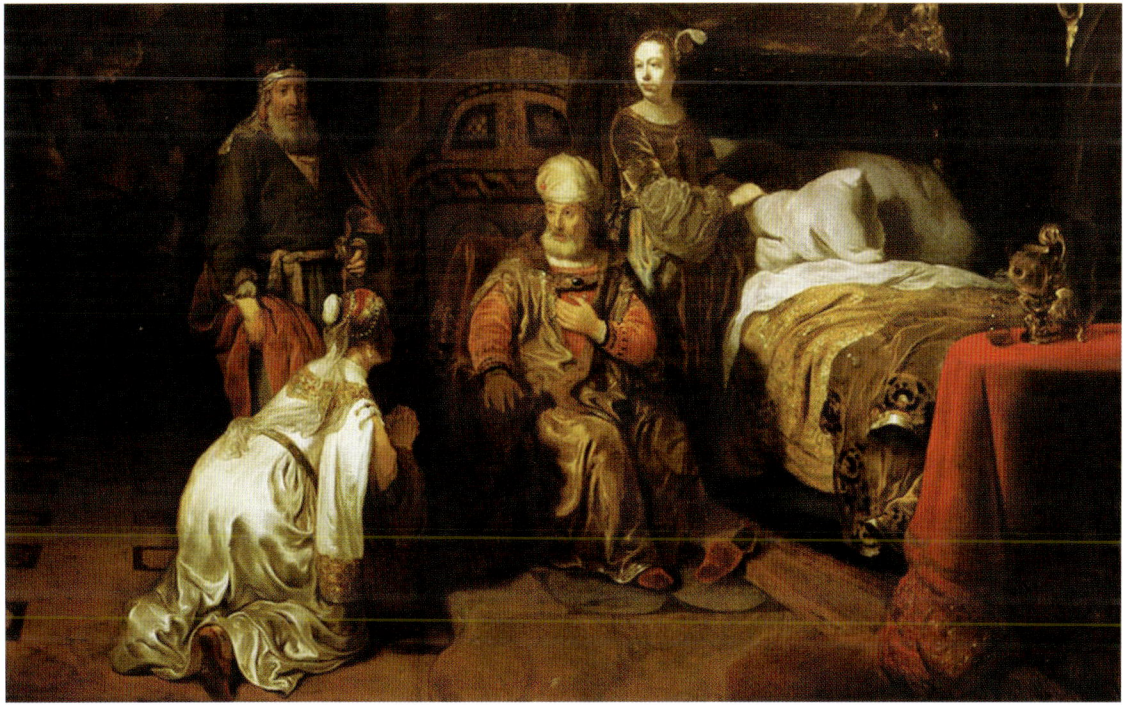

OPPOSITE: **St. Helena with her son the emperor Constantine, depicted incongruously in this painting by Cornelis Engebrechtsz (c.1500) as a Holy Roman emperor. Helena carries the True Cross, which legend tells she discovered in Jerusalem.**

POWER-SHARING WOMEN

Other women helped win thrones for their sons and then peacefully co-ruled with them. The third-century Roman Empire provided several opportunities for such power sharing, although the Roman populace was inclined to view dependence on a mother as 'unmanly'. Elagabulus was declared emperor in AD 218 thanks to the plotting of his grandmother Maesa and mother Soaemius. Soaemius continued to have such a strong sway on the government (Elagabulus was mainly interested in promoting the cult of a new god) that when Elagabulus was deposed in 222, Soaemius was killed along with him; their bodies mutilated and dragged through the streets. Mamaea, the mother of Severus Alexander, also ruled with him, and soldiers blamed him for his dependence and poor leadership, and condemned her greed. They too were overthrown, in 235, and killed together.

Some women were understandably unwilling to hand over power to an untried stripling after they themselves had successfully governed a great state for years. For example, Queen Dowager Xuan of Qin (d. 265 BC) ruled as regent for her son and held power for 41 years. Dowager Empress Deng Sui of the later Han similarly served as regent for 15 years until her death, emphatically refusing to hand over power. After Deng Sui's husband died in AD 106 without naming either of his sons as heir, Deng chose the baby for the throne, and when he died selected a 12-year-old grandson of her husband's in his place. She then adamantly refused to hand over power when the boy grew up, sentencing to death a man who petitioned her to relinquish power. Yet why should she have given up power? Deng Sui was a highly effective ruler who organized famine relief and vigorously combatted administrative corruption; only the view that the ruler ought to be male kept her hold on power insecure.

Women who held political power in their husbands' reigns were particularly unlikely to step aside gracefully for the next generation. This was true of the two greatest ladies of first-century Rome, Livia and Agrippina the Younger. Livia, as we have seen, had been Augustus Caesar's partner. When her son Tiberius came to power, he forcefully sidelined her, apparently resenting her superior grasp of Roman politics; she fought back through her political networks. More sensational was the fate of Agrippina the Younger (AD 15–59). She dominated her husband Claudius, and convinced him to adopt her own son Nero as his heir. Contemporaries thought she would do anything to assure Nero's succession, including perhaps poisoning Claudius. Tacitus reports that astrologers told Agrippina that Nero would become emperor and kill his mother, to which she is supposed to have responded 'He is welcome to kill me, as long as he becomes emperor.' Agrippina, a direct

OVERLEAF: **After Agrippina and her son Nero fell out, Nero tried several times to have his mother murdered. This 1874 painting by Gustav Wertheimer depicts how the emperor arranged to have Agrippina's ship collapse. The empress, a strong swimmer, survived the wreck.**

descendant of Augustus, thought she could control her son as she had her elderly husband, repeatedly stressing that he owed his position to her, but tensions soon arose over his choice of wife. Nero eventually expelled his mother from Rome, but apparently still fearing her political influence and 'fierceness,' he arranged her murder in AD 59.

The most bizarre case of a queen mother's dealings with her adult son is probably the tale of Musa, the principal wife of Phraates IV of Parthia. Musa was an Italian slave, a gift to the Parthian king from Augustus. She became queen, and she and her son poisoned Phraates in 2 BC when he refused to name the boy as heir. Musa and Phraates V then ruled jointly, and married to seal the deal. They held power until AD 4, when the Parthian nobles overthrew them for incest and patricide.

TRANSGRESSING SOCIAL NORMS

Throughout the ancient world, male authors readily believed that women schemed, seduced and deceived their way into power. What in a man was regarded as ambition or even 'destiny' in women was madness for power, and authors seemed determined to tell audiences of transgressive behaviour, the more outrageous the better. How many of the stories of evil or immoral ruling women are actually true, however, is impossible to uncover. Sometimes, we can gauge contemporary reactions to powerful women. The first female head of state in Asia was Queen Anula of Anuradhapura (present-day Sri Lanka). She started her career as a queen consort, but later took the throne herself and reigned for five years. Historical sources accuse her of poisoning at least five husbands, reportedly so that she could retain power herself. Eventually, the original king's kinsmen deposed Anula and burnt her alive in 44 BC, suggesting that they believed her to be a murderer.

Similarly, after Laodicé of Cappadocia's husband was killed in battle (131/130 BC) she became regent. She reputedly poisoned five of their six sons before they grew up in order to rule herself; the youngest was saved. The populace, outraged, joined together in rebellion and Laodicé was assassinated in c.126 BC. Were the children really poisoned,

BELOW: Statue of Queen Anula from the Avenue of Kings, Mihintale, Sri Lanka.

In the Seleucid Empire, Queen Laodike reportedly poisoned her weak husband Antiochus II, clearing the way to the throne for her own son by ordering the murder of the king's second wife and her son.

or did they just die, as children so frequently did in the premodern world? The accusation that powerful women were poisoners was bandied about in many regions and is impossible to prove or disprove.

Some women really do appear to have transgressed social norms to gain power or preserve their own position. In the Seleucid Empire, Queen Laodike reportedly poisoned her weak husband Antiochus II, clearing the way to the throne for her own son by ordering the murder of the king's second wife and her son. Cleopatra Thea, an Egyptian princess who became a Seleucid queen, reportedly killed her own son Seleucus V when he took the throne; Roman sources say she committed the deed personally. This Cleopatra met her end in c.121 BC when her younger son Antiochus VIII Grypus started demanding power; she tried to poison him, but he made her drink the cup instead. A particularly shocking case from late antiquity that appears well-attested involves Fausta, wife of Constantine the Great, the fourth-century Roman emperor. She effectively turned Constantine against Crispus, her stepson, by lying that the young man had made sexual advances to her. When Constantine found out the truth, he had Fausta murdered.

Sexual double standards were, of course, commonplace during antiquity. Even where polygyny was not the norm, a husband could simply repudiate his wife if he tired of her and enjoy as many mistresses as he pleased, while the wife was expected to be chaste. The mere rumour of sexual misconduct could make a powerful woman fall abruptly from grace. In the late Roman Empire, Eudocia, wife of Theodosius II, engaged in a sometimes-vicious rivalry with her sister-in-law Pulcheria for influence at court. Accusations of adultery finally drove her from court. Eudocia settled in the Holy Land, where her enormous wealth helped shape the religious landscape.

Inevitably, some women used their sexuality to garner power, either to gain influence over their husbands or to consolidate independent rule. The famous example of this is Cleopatra VII of Egypt. While she officially co-ruled with two successive brothers and then her young son (51–30 BC), Cleopatra won

ABOVE: **Cleopatra Thea issued a striking statement of her position as true ruler of the Seleucid Empire when she issued this tetradrachm giving her own profile precedence over that of her son Antiochus VIII Grypus.**

two of the greatest Romans of her age as lovers and protectors, Julius Caesar and Mark Antony. The Roman troops they commanded secured Cleopatra's position on the Egyptian throne for decades, although her marriage to Mark Antony and their claim to rule the east finally tipped the balance of Roman opinion against the couple, leading to their defeat in the Battle of Actium (31 BC) and suicide the next year. Perhaps Julia Berenice of Judea, a daughter of Herod Agrippa, learnt from Cleopatra VII's example. After several marriages, this Berenice became co-ruler with her brother Agrippa II. When the Romans conquered Judea, she became lover to the Roman commander Titus, holding that position for 13 years. When he became emperor in AD 79, Titus wanted to marry his Judean love, but public uproar at the idea of him marrying a Jewess who was years older led him to banish her to Gaul instead.

THE PERILS OF INDEPENDENT POWER

When a woman gained independent power, she had to be very careful about who she married, especially since droves of men hoped to rule through her. Regents rarely remarried, but sovereign queens faced the biological imperative to produce heirs. Sometimes a queen by right of inheritance found herself at loggerheads with her husband as he tried to dominate her. Such was the case with Cartimandua of the Brigantes (northern Britain), who ruled AD 41–60.

OPPOSITE: **Elizabeth Taylor playing Cleopatra VII of Egypt in the classic 1963 film** *Cleopatra*, **directed by Joseph L. Mankiewicz.**

LEFT: **'The Battle of Actium,' part of a tapestry series presenting the story of Caesar and Cleopatra, woven in Brussels, c.1600 in the workshop of Willem van Leefdael.**

The Roman poet Virgil's retelling of Dido's death describes the queen killing herself from despair after her lover Aeneas abandons her to follow his destiny as Rome's founder. Her tragedy was a popular theme in art, as in this statue by Claude-Augustin Cayot (1711).

She ruled jointly with her husband Venutius, but he opposed her pro-Roman policy and tried to overthrow her. With Roman support, Cartimandua prevailed, only to abandon the Brigantes and run off with a lover.

The Egyptian Neferusobek, last of her dynasty, decided on marriage; she might have been trying to avoid favouring any one noble faction when she married a commoner and elevated him to the throne. The result was public fury and a civil war that gave the Hyksos an opportunity to invade. The later female pharaoh Sobekneferu charted a safer course by never marrying, although it meant the Twelfth Dynasty died with her.

The notion that the heiress to a throne was a lawful prize for whoever could seize and marry her led to the demise of several independent queens of the ancient world. Dido of Carthage, although a largely legendary figure, is instructive. Her original story tells that she led her supporters to found the city-state of Carthage in 785 BC, but then a local chief tried to force her into marriage. To avoid handing over control of her people to a foreigner, she publicly committed suicide. More historical is the second of two Sassanian Persian queens who ruled in their own right successively in the chaos after the death of their father Khusrau II in AD 628. The first, Boran, ruled for at least 16 months, followed by her half-sister, Azarmigduxt. However, Azarmigduxt did not last long because she refused to marry a noble and killed him for his presumption; the man's son then captured, blinded and killed the queen.

The worst indignation and most lurid accusations were reserved for women who transgressed religiously, especially by advocating worship of the wrong deity. When Jezebel married Ahab, king of Israel, she introduced the worship of Baal and Asherah and purged the prophets of Yahweh. In the ensuing rebellion Ahab, their son and finally Jezebel herself were killed; she was thrown from a window and left for the dogs to eat.

In a similar vein, Jezebel's near-contemporary Athaliah of Judah is accused in Hebrew scripture of seizing the throne after her son Ahaziah died in battle in 840 BC, killing all of her grandsons except one who was hidden away. Her true crime, however, was to introduce the worship of Baal, and for this Athaliah was overthrown and executed in 839 or 837 BC. By contrast, as we will see in the next chapter, support of the right religion could enhance a ruling woman's power.

LEFT: Gustave Doré catches the drama of Jezebel's death in this 1885 engraving, one of many biblical scenes that the artist illustrated.

POWER AND INFLUENCE IN THE EARLY MIDDLE AGES

In the early Middle Ages (c.400–1000) the patterns of where and when women could hold power shifted from what we have seen in the ancient world. However, it remained constant in most regions that women did not inherit crowns when males of the royal family were available. New factors also emerged that further limited women's access to royal power. In Europe, the Germanic states that succeeded the Roman Empire did not enjoy Rome's tradition of women playing a public role; as a result, few women held on to power for long. Nonetheless, being part of a warrior society did not always limit women, as we will see in the case of the Liu Dynasty, nomadic in origin, which ruled a kingdom in northern China for several centuries.

OPPOSITE: **French artist Jean-Joseph Benjamin-Constant imagined Byzantine Empress Theodora as a darkly forbidding figure in this 1887 painting. Notions of Theodora have been shaded ever since the sixth century by Procopius' wildly negative description of the entertainer-turned-empress.**

RIGHT: **Did Judith, second wife of the Carolingian emperor Louis the Pious, really pester him to give a share of the empire to her son Charles (the Bald)? This nineteenth-century engraver certainly thought so.**

OPPOSITE: **Bertha (or Bertrada) of Laon, mother of Charlemagne, was later known as 'Bertha Broad-Foot.' No trace of abnormal foot size appears in this nineteenth-century cast of a thirteenth-century statue, on display at Versailles.**

BELOW: **Queen Clothilde was canonized as a saint in large part because it was believed she was responsible for the conversion of her husband, the Merovingian king Clovis, to Catholic Christianity. Here, she is shown presiding over his baptism.**

One of the most striking features of the early medieval period is that a number of religious orthodoxies enshrined cultural notions of female inferiority as god-given truth. With the triumph of Christianity in much of Europe came religious affirmation that women should be subject to men, that they should not presume to teach men and that women are uniquely prone to temptation and sin. The Qur'an, while accepting that women are equally able to obtain God's favour as men, also states that God placed women under the guardianship of men, making it likely that any woman holding power would be regarded as an aberration. In China and the lands under Chinese cultural influence, the growing centrality of Confucian thought firmly demanded the subordination of women. Only in Japan, where Shinto and Buddhism religions remained dominant, were women sovereigns apparently accepted without question.

Nonetheless, new religious orthodoxies also offered opportunities for women to gain access to power. A number of European queens are regarded as central in prompting the conversion of their kingdoms, usually when they came to their husbands as part of prestigious marriage alliances. Thus the Merovingian queen Clothilde (d. 544) stood up to her husband Clovis, insisting that her sons be baptized and influencing her husband to the point that, in a crucial battle, he prayed to 'Clothild's god' for help, promising conversion in return for victory. Similarly, the Merovingian princess Bertha, who became queen of Kent, helped introduce Christianity to southern England shortly before 600, and the Byzantine princess Anna brought Christianity with her when she married Vladimir of Kiev in the late tenth century.

A powerful woman could win meaningful support by sponsoring a particular religion or religious sect. Queen Sóndók Yówang of Silla, who ruled part of what is present-day Korea (632–47), oversaw the introduction of Zen Buddhism to her kingdom, building several Buddhist temples that provided a visible sign of her power and won the gratitude of Buddhist subjects. Empress Irene of Byzantium is a saint of the Greek Orthodox Church (despite killing her own son) because she restored the veneration of holy images to her empire. Notably, Wu Zetian, the one sovereign woman in Chinese imperial history, used omens purposefully to consolidate her rule, including some that were clearly concocted, such as the 'finding' of a stone predicting the coming of a 'wise mother' to rule. Wu later claimed that she was a reincarnation of the Buddhist goddess Maitreya and also linked herself to Dao philosophy and the goddess Nügua. In other words, she resisted the dominant Confucianism by patronizing and associating with minority religions, especially Buddhism.

THE NATURE OF WOMEN'S AUTHORITY

Although most Eurasian religions frowned on women in authority, Christianity in particular devised a signal way to mark out queens as special recipients of God's favour and protection, elevating them out of the limitations imposed on the rest of their sex – coronation. First in Visigothic Spain, kings were anointed with holy oil, imitating the unction of the biblical kings of Israel, transporting them ritually into a sacred space as special servants of God. We first know of a queen receiving a similar consecration in 754, when the Frankish Bertha, wife of the Carolingian usurper Pepin, was anointed and crowned alongside her husband and sons, demonstrating the elevation of a whole lineage to royal rank.

The oldest actual surviving ceremony was designed for the unction of Judith, daughter of Charles the Bald, when she married King Aethelwulf of Wessex in 856. Her marriage to an older man with adult sons clearly called for special protections, and the ritual assured that Judith had a rank above that of any other woman in England. The ritual also included special prayers for the queen's fruitfulness, implicitly stressing that the children of an anointed queen have a unique status

as heirs. The custom of anointing queens had spread widely in Europe by the tenth century, significantly changing the nature of queenship from 'just' being a king's wife to having a recognized role in the right order of things.

As in antiquity, queens everywhere derived not only protection but also invaluable political support and leverage from their birth families. The vast majority of kings chose wives of noble or royal blood, although Frankish Merovingian kings were exceptional in marrying slave women. Much more typical was China in the later Han Dynasty, where most empresses came from powerful clans that were jockeying for power at court. Such women, whether in Asia or in Europe, had ready-made support networks that had often been

RIGHT: Empress Liu, powerful regent of the Chinese Song Dynasty, appears in this later painting as a placid elderly woman – belying the reputation she had in life.

ABOVE: **Wealtheow in the Anglo-Saxon epic *Beowulf* appears as the ideal Germanic queen, welcoming warriors to Hrothgar's hall and bestowing costly gifts on heroes. The film *Beowulf* (2007) takes many liberties with the plot, building Wealtheow (played by Robin Wright Penn) into a more significant character.**

cultivated over generations. In this way, if the queen or empress came to public power, she could count on supportive kinsmen who were accustomed to authority.

The lack of a powerful family was a major liability to Empress Liu, who was an entertainer – a hand drummer – when she attracted the Chinese emperor's attention. Liu was named empress and came to power in 1020 after her husband fell ill; when he died in 1022, she became regent for his son by another wife. Officials repeatedly asked Liu to step down and prevented her from using the imperial pronoun *zhen* (the masculine royal 'I'). Despite their efforts, she kept power until her death in 1033, but her position would have been eased by a family network. In Europe at about the same time, France's Carolingian dynasty ended after the last male of the family was passed over in 987 because his wife was considered too low-born to be a queen.

Whether high- or low-born, queens had access to wealth, and wealth procured power. Women usually brought a dowry to marriage, but more important was the marriage settlement typical in both east and west. Lands and incomes were assigned to royal brides, with which they paid the expenses of their households and purchased loyalties. Such settlements could be enormous, allowing queens to engage in extensive patronage as well as presenting themselves sumptuously to win public respect. Beyond their personal incomes, queens also had varying access to their husbands' wealth – hardly surprising in early medieval Europe, where the king's treasure was likely kept in a chest at the foot of their bed. Generally, in Europe, the

queen controlled the royal household; Danish queen Wealtheow in the poem *Beowulf* demonstrates the ideal of hospitality and generosity queens were expected to display.

SUCCESSES AND FAILURES OF FEMALE SOVEREIGNTY

In Japanese, the term *tennō*, usually translated as 'emperor', is actually ungendered and simply means 'heavenly sovereign.' The lack of grammatical gender seems especially appropriate since Japan in the period 593–770 saw eight male rulers and six females, two of whom returned to the throne for a second reign after their abdication. All of these female emperors inherited from a male relative. The ease with which they took office can probably be attributed to Buddhism – which probably also explains why the Bhauma-Kara dynasty of eastern India accepted five female sovereigns in the eighth to tenth centuries, as did several other Indian kingdoms. Buddhism was officially recognized in Japan in 594 with the ascension of the Buddhist nun Suiko, the first ruler to hold the title tennō.

Several of these female emperors enjoyed notable reigns and influenced the course of Japanese history. Suiko, who succeeded her brothers and ruled from 592 to 628, is credited with establishing the complete supremacy of the ruler over Japan's people. She embraced Chinese influences selectively, sent Japan's first embassy to China and adopted the Chinese bureaucratic system and calendar. Gemmei, who became tennō in 708 after her son died, also proved very able. She had the ancient customs of Japan compiled and was responsible

院天皇

ねむし浮き

まきの

ことも

のちも

はほふ

むまや

for moving the capital to Nara. Gemmei-tennō abdicated after six years on the throne – in favour of her daughter Genshō rather than her son. Unfortunately for the future of women's rule in Japan, the last of this remarkable run of female sovereigns, Kōken-tennō, was less successful. More interested in religion than ruling, she was dominated by a Buddhist priest named Dōkyō, who might have been her lover, to the point of nearly abdicating in his favour. Japan's nobles forced Kōken to abdicate in 758 after nine years of rule, although she was restored to the throne six years later. The nobles swore that no other woman would ever rule – and in fact there were only two female tennō in later centuries, both of whom abdicated as soon as a male of the family reached adulthood.

Korea, although more influenced by Confucianism than was Japan, also produced two sovereign queens in the seventh century and another in the ninth. In both cases, Chinese influence made their rule more difficult. Queen Sóndók came to the throne of Silla despite strong noble opposition in 632. Sóndók was socially progressive and worked especially to improve care of the needy. However, the Chinese emperor refused to acknowledge her and when she sought aid in a crisis, he said he would only give military assistance if he could also provide a man of his own Tang dynasty to rule Silla. Sóndók weathered that storm only to face a rebellion by her own officials in 647; she triumphed again, but died soon after. Her heir was a female cousin, Chindók Yówang, who ruled from 647 to 654. She continued a policy of alliance with China and accepted strong Chinese cultural influence. With the triumph of Confucianism in Korea, later Confucian scholars proclaimed the rule of these women to be an aberration.

China itself has only had one female sovereign – and one would-be woman emperor – in its history. In both cases, the women involved pitted themselves directly against Confucian orthodoxy. The first did so by radically transgressive means: Chen Shuozhen was leader of a peasant rebellion that broke out in 653. Claiming to have magic powers and that she had been turned into a man when visiting heaven, she declared herself emperor Wenija. Her 'reign' lasted only two months before she was killed in battle.

Wu Zetian declared herself emperor – adopting the sovereign title *huangdi* rather than the term *huanghou* used for empresses.

Wu Zetian (624–705), who ruled China in her own name from 690 to 705 as the only emperor of her self-created dynasty (the Zhou), followed a more conventional path to power. Wu started her career as an imperial concubine, but rose to the rank of empress when she bore an heir. Her husband, Gaozang, suffered a series of strokes that left him incapacitated; he delegated power to his dynamic wife. When Gaozang died in 683, Wu's son became emperor, but she soon deposed him in favour of his younger brother – evidence that Wu Zetian held true power in China. When the younger son abdicated in 690 (the official reason given was that a phoenix had been sighted), Wu Zetian, by then 65 years old, declared herself emperor – adopting the sovereign title *huangdi* rather than the term *huanghou* used for empresses.

Wu's patronage of Buddhists and Daoists helped keep her on the throne until 705, when conspirators took advantage of a long illness to depose her and restore her elder son to the throne. The female emperor's successful reign inspired both her daughter and granddaughter to strive for sovereignty, although both failed. Confucian administrator-scholars were determined that no future woman would have as much power as Wu; of the 17 emperors of the Tang Dynasty after her, the empresses of only two had significant power, and 11 did not name an empress at all. Over time, Wu herself suffered from historical erasure. Some Confucian scholars removed her from historical sources altogether, while others transformed her from a legitimate emperor to a usurper. By the Ming era, Wu Zetian had become a popular figure in pornographic fiction.

Beyond Eurasia, we have tantalizing hints of female sovereignty in the early medieval period. One of the most striking examples is Dihya, a Berber queen who led resistance to the Muslim conquest of the Magreb in the later seventh century.

BELOW: A stark testimony to the controversial nature of Wu Zetian's reign. Wu erected a stele at her husband's tomb and wrote an inscription, but left the stele for her own tomb blank, expecting her successor to provide the epitaph. Instead, the 'Wordless Stele' was left blank, a first sign of China's effort to erase the memory of Wu.

A military as well as religious leader, Dihya won a notable victory over an Islamic army in the Battle of Meskiana (698); Arabic sources acknowledge her influence over her people by naming her al-Kahina, 'the soothsayer.' Dihya ruled for five years before her defeat and death in the Battle of Tabarka in c.703.

UNNATURAL MOTHER OR SAINT?

LEFT: In this copy of a Byzantine coin, Empress Irene and her son Constantine VI appear almost to be wrestling to control of the sceptre, the eighteenth-century artist perhaps purposely emphasizing the tension that led to Irene's seizure of power and the death of Constantine.

Irene of Athens (c.752–803) was the daughter of a prominent noble family who married Byzantine emperor Leo IV. When her husband died in 780, she became regent for their 10-year-old son Constantine VI. As regent, Empress Irene reversed Leo's religious policies and strongly supported the veneration of holy images. This widely popular decision gave Irene leverage when her son first demanded she step down; she had him whipped and forced him to acknowledge her as senior ruler. Late in 790, Constantine was able to seize personal power and imprison his mother, but within a year he bowed to pressure and recalled her as co-ruler. The pair co-ruled for five tense years, Constantine becoming increasingly unpopular for his lackadaisical attitude towards governance and threats to restore iconoclasm. Finally, in August 797, Irene staged a coup. She had her son seized, imprisoned and blinded – after which he soon died.

From 797 until she herself was overthrown in 802, Irene was sovereign, even occasionally using the masculine title basileus (emperor) to underline her authority. She surmounted the challenges of ruling as a woman in the strictly gendered Byzantine world by relying heavily on eunuchs as officials, which gave her access to the public space normally denied to women. Irene's competence is most visible in the sheer fact of her political survival – she held effective power for 22 years despite the resistance of five brothers-in-law, a son and army, plus a bureaucratic leadership that never really supported her. Although Irene died in exile the year after being deposed, she lives on as a saint of the Greek Orthodox Church for her restoration of icons.

Another African sovereign woman who fought in the name of religion was Judith of Abyssinia, who ruled for 40 years in the tenth-century kingdom of Axum and became the subject of many later legends. During her reign, she launched a major persecution of Christians, and is credited with killing thousands.

For this period, we also have evidence of a few ruling women in the Americas, known thanks to inscriptions on Maya monuments. The Maya produced at least three female kings who ruled in their own right – Kanal-Ikal and Zac-Kuk in the kingdom of Palenque and Wac-Chanil-Ahau in Naranjo. We know most about Kanal-Ikal, who ascended the throne in 583 when either her father or brother died and there was no male heir; she ruled for at least 20 years. Wac-Chanil-Ahau (d. 741) appears on monuments as a warrior king. Our knowledge is limited by the brevity of inscriptions, but scholars have hypothesized that women's position in Maya society became more public in the seventh and eighth centuries, giving royal women a role in rituals and allowing some to take on traditional men's roles when conditions were right.

ABOVE: This funerary mask was found in the Tomb of the Red Queen in Temple XIII in the Maya city of Palenque. It was perhaps the tomb of Lady Ix Tz'akbu Ajaw and dates to the seventh century.

FEMALE SOVEREIGNTY IN MEDIEVAL EUROPE

In contrast to later eras, the region most adamantly opposed to female sovereignty in the early Middle Ages was Europe. This can probably be attributed to the warrior ethos of the Germanic successor states, which placed a strong emphasis on having an adult male ruler who could lead his people personally in battle. For example, when the Lombard king Authari died in

The cousin soon deposed and imprisoned Amalasuintha, and in May 535 had her assassinated.

590, Queen Theodelinda was regarded so highly that she was given a political role. The nobles did not give her sovereignty, however; instead, they asked her to choose one of them as husband and promised they would give him the crown. Nearly four centuries later, Queen Adelheid, a young woman when her husband Lothar died, had a blood right to the crown of Lombardy in her own name, not to mention the rights of her young daughter Emma. However, an ambitious noble seized the throne for himself, imprisoning Adelheid, who eventually escaped; her second husband, Otto I of Germany, was able to claim Lombardy by right of his wife.

In only two cases did European women actually obtain sovereign status in the period 500–1000. The first was ultimately tragic. The Goth Theoderic, who ruled Italy from 493 to 526, only had a daughter – Amalasuintha (c.495–535). She was not intended to rule, although she received an excellent Roman-style education. Instead, Amalasuintha was to transmit rule to her husband Eutheric, but he died three years before Theoderic. The throne was therefore left to Theoderic's 10-year-old grandson, with Amalasuintha as his guardian and regent. When the boy died in 534, Amalasuintha tried to hold on to power, but found it impossible to rule without a man. Instead, she named a cousin as co-ruler, although they did not marry and she demanded recognition as senior partner. This backfired spectacularly; the cousin soon deposed and imprisoned Amalasuintha, and in May 535 had her assassinated. Ultimately, the Gothic aristocracy was not prepared to accept a woman's rule.

OPPOSITE: A fantasy bust of the Ostrogothic queen Amalasuintha. In reality, Theodoric's daughter did not attempt to command Gothic troops; her need for a male general led to her overthrow and murder.

BELOW: In the TV series *The Last Kingdom* (2015–22), based on the novels of Bernard Cornwell, Aethelflaed of Mercia, played by Millie Brady, has been developed as a major character, building on the few contemporary references we have to her reign.

This leaves Aethelflaed (c.870–918) – 'lady of the Mercians' – as the only truly successful sovereign woman of early medieval Europe. Aethelflaed was a daughter of Alfred the Great of Wessex. Alfred established loose overlordship over the formerly independent kingdom of Mercia thanks to his vigorous fight against the Vikings. He married Aethelflaed to the ealdorman (prefect) of Mercia and she was the effective ruler of Mercia well before her husband's death in 911. After his death, her own dynamic personality, as well as her descent from the Mercian royal house on her mother's side, allowed her to continue ruling in her own name. Aethelflaed gained a major military reputation, not only extending the Wessex system of fortified refuges to Mercia but also by campaigning against the Vikings with her brother, King Edward the Elder of Wessex. Edward was content to work in alliance with his sister. When she died in 918, however, he consigned Aethelflaed's daughter to a convent and incorporated Mercia into his own expanding kingdom.

BELOW: An evil stepmother? Aelfthryth, the second wife of King Edgar of England, was suspected of arranging the murder of her stepson Edward so her own child could take the throne. Here, she is shown duplicitously sending Edward to where her henchmen were waiting to murder him.

REGENCY – THE SUREST ROAD TO POWER

As in the ancient world, royal mothers of the early Middle Ages were regarded as the most natural guardians of minor sons, despite anomalies such as Irene of Byzantium and Wu Zetian. Royal mothers rose to power when biological factors, especially the premature death of kings, allowed it, rather than following any recognizable pattern. Some periods seemed particularly regent-prone, however. Strikingly, for part of the 980s, queen-regents ruled most of Christian western Europe – Aelfthryth in England, Theophanu in the German Empire, Emma in France and Beatrice in semi-independent Lotharingia. Even the caliphate of Cordoba had a woman regent, Subh – the only Muslim woman known to have held official public power in this era.

Such a cluster of regencies points to Europe's greater political stability, which allowed children to survive on the throne. By contrast, in seventh-century Visigothic Spain, minority rule inevitably led to political crisis, with the boy-king murdered or deposed in short order.

While a mother was the most common guardian of children on the throne, often at the express will of the preceding ruler, her choice was not inevitable, and when a widow was named as regent, conditions might be imposed. Such was the case when the Byzantine empress Theodora became regent in 842 for her two-year-old son; her husband in his will imposed a eunuch court official as co-regent. Apparently the two worked well together – well enough to rouse the suspicions of the young emperor, who at the age of about 15 arranged the murder of the eunuch with his uncle's help. The youth apparently believed a story that the two co-regents planned to depose and blind him in order to hold on to power, and was unwilling to risk the fate of Constantine VI. The dowager empress was formally deposed from her regency soon thereafter.

Two European examples illustrate other factors that could be involved. When the aptly nicknamed King Louis the Child inherited the East Frankish kingdom in c.900, a bishop received care of the kingdom rather than his mother Ota, probably because Ota had been publicly accused of adultery shortly before her husband's death. Even without suspicion of wrongdoing, sometimes a mother was poorly placed to serve as regent. Thus Elvira was a highly successful regent of León in the tenth century for her nephew Ramiro III, in preference to the boy's mother, who was foreign-born and lacked the influence Elvira enjoyed as a daughter of the ruling dynasty (she had been at court almost constantly in her brother's reign). Additionally, the fact that Elvira was abbess of a great royal

POSSESSION IS NINE PARTS OF THE LAW

A child king was, by a global legal fiction, the ruler. Royal commands were issued in the child's name and the pretence was maintained that he was in control, no matter how young. This gave the person with actual control of the child an incalculable advantage, acting as the real power behind the throne. Nowhere can this be seen more compellingly than in the minority of Otto III of Germany. Otto, already crowned as co-king with his father, inherited the throne late in 983 when he was only three years old. His mother Theophanu and grandmother Adelheid were both in Italy, where Otto II had died. A royal cousin, Duke Henry 'the Quarrelsome' of Bavaria, immediately took charge of the boy, either to rule in his name or perhaps as a stepping stone to seize the throne for himself.

Theophanu and Adelheid worked together in this crisis for the Ottonian dynasty. They crossed the Alps, pulled together a coalition of supporters and in time confronted Duke Henry with such an overwhelming military coalition that he surrendered the child to their care without a fight. Theophanu was then able to rule as regent until her death, succeeded in that office by her mother-in-law, the redoubtable Adelheid.

Despite the dynamism of these two imperial women, some acts continued to require the presence of the child king. For example, six-year-old Otto was dressed in miniature armour and taken to war against the Slavs, since only the actual king could fittingly receive the homage of the duke of Poland, who was taking part in the campaign.

When Theophanu was so securely in control that she felt able to leave her son for a time and journey to Italy it was exceptional. Without Otto's presence, she could not issue documents in his name and on at least two occasions her secretaries penned charters in the name of the masculinized 'Theophanius,' dating them from her own consecration as empress.

BELOW: One of the few contemporary depictions of the Greek-born empress Theophanu, this engraving is from the front cover of the *Golden Gospels of Echternach.*

convent assured that she would not take a husband who might try to usurp the throne. That the dowager queen became a nun under Elvira's authority suggests that the former had lost a power struggle.

A grandmother might also serve as regent if the mother were no longer in the picture. In the eighth century, Plectrude, wife of the Carolingian Pepin II, fought her stepson Charles Martel for control of Francia on behalf of her grandson. She lost, but the fact that it took three battles for Charles to defeat her demonstrates the breadth of her political alliances and influence. Adelheid of the German Empire was a more successful grandmother. She assumed the regency for the young Otto III after his mother Theophanu died in 991 and controlled the government without opposition until Otto came of age.

The Frankish Merovingian dynasty produced more than its fair share of regencies, thanks to the fratricidal tendencies of the male family members as well as a number of premature deaths from accidents or illness. Unlike other early medieval kingdoms in Europe, the prestige of the royal bloodline allowed minors to inherit. The most notorious of the women who served as regents was Brunhild (c.534–613), whose son Childebert became king of Austrasia at the age of five. The mother continued to play a strong role in government after Childebert came of age, completely overshadowing her son's wife. When Childebert died, aged only 26, Brunhild became regent again – and a third time for her great-grandson in 613. Brunhild's long ascendancy was marked by a bitter feud with the neighbouring Merovingian-ruled

BELOW: The reign, and especially the brutal death, of the Austrasian queen mother Brunnhild has fascinated people ever since the seventh century. This 1825 print shows her execution, dragged to death by a wild horse.

ABOVE: **Balthild won popular acclaim during her time as regent, not just for support of churches but also for the charitable activities she personally carried out.**

kingdom of Neustria. She met her end when a coalition of her own nobles banded with their enemies to prevent her third regency. After being defeated in battle, the elderly Brunhild was killed, tied by her hair, one arm and one leg to an unbroken horse and dragged to her death.

More benign is the story of Balthild of Neustria, an Anglo-Saxon slave who became queen and regent for her son Chlothar III. During the seven years of her regency (657–664), Balthild proved herself a good political leader, launching significant political and religious reforms and paving the way to a reunification of the Kingdom of the Franks. She owed much of her success to the good relations she cultivated with the clergy. After her regency, the queen mother retired to the convent she had founded at Chelles, and became recognized as a saint.

CHINESE EMPRESS-REGENTS

Even in China, despite the strong reaction to the reign of Wu Zetian, women could occasionally take political leadership as regents. An interesting example

耗資逾一億台幣的歷史正劇，完全展現北魏的史實風貌
中國歷史上第一位政績卓著的女改革家

北魏 冯太后

Empress Feng of the Northern Wei Dynasty

LEFT: **Jacklyn Wu portrayed Dowager Empress Feng of the Northern Wei Dynasty in a 42-episode popular TV series in 2006.**

is Chu Suanzi (d. 384) of the Eastern Jin Dynasty. She bore no sons herself, but as empress took precedence over her husband's concubines, even those who gave birth to potential heirs. Chu Suanzi outlived her husband by 40 years, ruling as regent for three of his successors. Her approach to holding court catered to Confucian sensibilities and cultural norms about behaviour appropriate to women. In formal audiences, she held the emperor in her arms, visibly emphasizing her role as surrogate mother and guardian. Few saw her, however, because Chu Suanzi was the first dowager regent to seat herself behind a curtain when dealing with courtiers, a practice that became standard in the Song Dynasty.

The Northern Wei Dynasty also produced several dowager empress-regents. Empress Feng (442–490) did not initially enjoy a government role when her husband died in 465 and her 11-year-old stepson inherited. However, in 466 she made herself regent in a coup. Feng was forced to abdicate the office within the year, but did not give up hope of power. A disagreement with the emperor (who had officially retired but controlled the government of his young son behind the scenes) led Feng to arrange his assassination, and in 476 she became regent again for the new boy-emperor. Feng ruled as virtual emperor, and even after her stepson came of age the new emperor carefully deferred to her until her death in 490.

Empress Ling (d. 528) of the Northern Wei went even further in her bid for power. She was never married to the emperor, but received the title 'empress dowager' and gained the regency when her son became emperor. Ling ruled this Chinese state as regent from 515 to 520 and regained power from her brother-in-law to rule again in 525–58. Dowager Empress Ling insisted on using terminology and administrative forms reserved for emperors; she was addressed as 'your majesty' and issued edicts. Most jarringly for contemporaries, she emulated the Han empress Lü by using

RIGHT: The women of the nomadic Khitan people played a larger role in public affairs than their Chinese neighbours. Here, a group of Khitan women are carrying out domestic tasks, which of course remained the main function of most female members of the tribe.

Chengtian accompanied her husband on military expeditions and had also been left in charge when he was absent on campaigns.

the *zhen* pronoun, the first-person singular 'I' that was unique to emperors. Ling even performed imperial sacrifices. Nonetheless, Ling's reign was not very successful; administrators considered her excessively lenient and her reign was punctuated by rebellion and government corruption. Her rule ended when her now-adult son ordered the execution of her reputed lover. In revenge, Ling had her son poisoned, and in retaliation a general captured and drowned Ling in the Yellow River.

The most prominent female regents of early medieval China were in the Liao Dynasty, which ruled a substantial area of northeastern China and the steppe from 907 to 1125. The rulers were nomadic Khitan and combined steppe and Chinese ruling methods, which worked both to the advantage and disadvantage of women. For example, Khitan women often played an active military role. Empress Yingtian (878–953) established the precedent for women's rule. During her husband Abaoji's lifetime, Yingtian campaigned with him, commanding her own fighting force, which she once used to save the emperor from an ambush. When Abaoji died suddenly in 926, Yingtian was expected either to marry his younger brother or to die with her husband. She refused to do either; instead, she cut off her right hand and placed it in the dead emperor's coffin. She then insisted on the succession of her second son as ruler, despite her husband's preference for the elder, and ruled as his regent. It is hardly surprising that when the new emperor grew up he remained very obedient to his strong-willed mother.

Dowager Empress Chengtian (953–1009) of the Liao Dynasty followed in her predecessor's footsteps. She took charge of the government when her husband died in 982. Like Yingtian, Chengtian had accompanied her husband on military expeditions and had also been left in charge when he was absent on campaigns, so she came to official power with considerable experience. To establish her authority more firmly, she performed at least three 'rebirth ceremonies' in the period 984–86 (ascending emperors normally carried out the ritual once). In 986, a Song army invaded Liao territory,

BELOW: This funerary garment resembles those found in the tombs of Liao princesses from the tenth century.

ABOVE: **In the Oval Palace Tablet, Mayan queen Zac-Kuk offers the crown to her son Pakal (seventh century).**

apparently sensing weakness in a period of women's rule. However, Chengtian took the field against them, personally commanding a 10,000-strong cavalry force, and completely defeated the invaders.

The dowager empress was responsible for sweeping administrative reforms, including more equitable tax collection and comprehensive steps to prevent administrative abuse. Particularly striking was the attention she paid to the sedentary agricultural population, instead of favouring the nomadic Khitan. Chengtian's position was so strong that she continued as effective ruler until her death in 1009. The Liao showed particularly profound respect for their mothers. When Dowager Empress Yingtian was dying, her son Emperor Deguang refused to eat and waited on her during her final illness; he then erected a stele honouring her merit and declared her birthday a national holiday.

SHARING IN RULE

Many effective regents had already served an apprenticeship by playing an active role in government during their husband's reign. Few were as exceptional as Liao empress Yingtian, who, when she joined her husband on military expeditions, directly commanded 5,000 horsemen, drawn from her own lands. In 916, she personally led an army to suppress a rebellion when her husband was away. Her on-the-job training also included more routine tasks of governance, such as receiving foreign embassies alongside her husband.

Women beyond Liao China continued to share rule with their adult sons. When women sometimes 'abdicated' from regency, it should be understood as simply a nod to cultural notions of female propriety, rather than any real intention to retire from political life. The reign of the Mayan female king of Palenque, Zac-Kuk, should probably be similarly understood . After she inherited the throne from her uncle, Zac-Kuk ruled from 612 to 615, but then abdicated when her son turned 12. Nonetheless, she continued as co-ruler for the next 25 years, until her death in 640. Although sources fail us, it is not difficult to imagine mature women continuing to exert influence over their adult children.

An interesting example from the Islamic world is Khayzuran (d. 789), wife of the Abbasid caliph al-Mahdi. The caliph cared more for hunting than governing, so for the decade before his death in 785 Khayzuran conducted much of the work of government. She held audiences and made important political decisions, maintaining her own bureaucracy and even having gold coins issued in her name. All were unprecedented achievements in Muslim society. Upon al-Mahdi's death, Khayzuran preserved the throne for her elder son, al-Hadi, until he could reach Baghdad. Nonetheless, al-Hadi tried to keep her out of government, threatening to behead anyone who sought her influence. The young caliph died after a 14-month-long reign; contemporaries believed Khayzuran had had him murdered, possibly suffocated by his own concubines. The dowager enjoyed much better relations with her younger son, Harun al-Rashid; she and Harun's wife Zubeida worked together on many public works, including the creation of a water supply system for the sacred precinct in Mecca. When Khayzuran died in 789, Harun broke tradition by publicly mourning her.

In western Europe, where early medieval monarchies were a household affair, visible evidence of wives participating in government seldom appears. Some Roman emperors in the ancient world had named their wives on coins, but European kings never did. Commemorating rulers in statuary had died out, so we do not have that valuable signal of female ruler's importance. Artists only started depicting queens again in the tenth century, and then only occasionally, for example in the Byzantine-inspired ivory plaque that celebrates the marriage of the Greek princess Theophanu to Otto II of Germany.

Royal women only appear in the sources if they did something extraordinary – or in charters. Royal

BELOW: **This ivory plaque celebrates the marriage of Theophanu and the German emperor Otto II. Note that while Otto has pride of place at Christ's right hand, the two figures of Theophanu and Otto are of equal size, with equally elaborate clothing and crowns.**

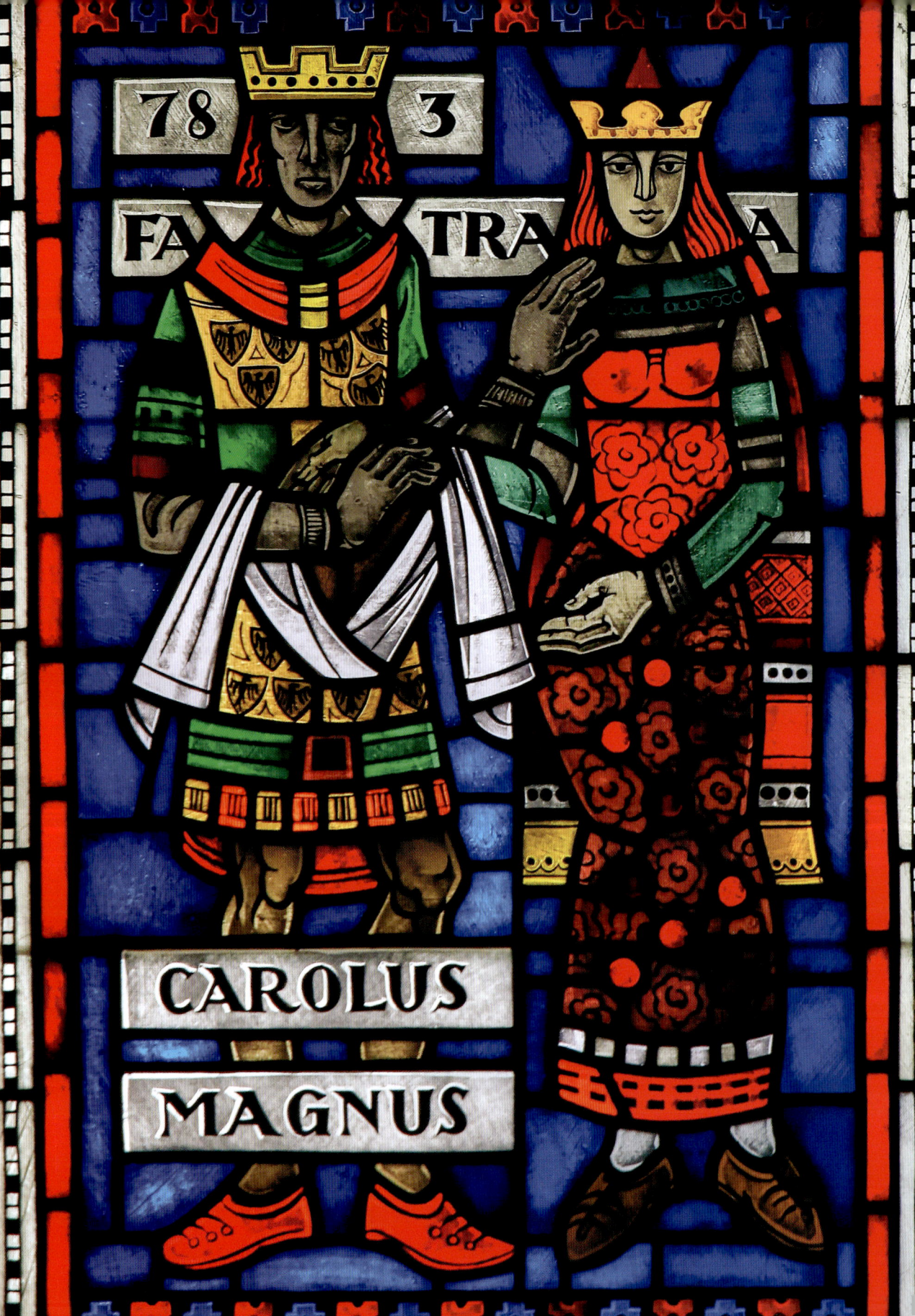

charters contain vital markers of women's influence and participation in government. When listed as witness to royal gifts, we can see that the queen was present, and can gauge her importance by her position on the witness list. Even better, when the queen is described as intervening to request a gift or favour, we can sometimes uncover a whole web of friendships and dependence. For example, Cynethryth, wife of Offa of Mercia at the end of the eighth century, is revealed as powerful above all through her witnessing of many charters. She even had coinage issued in her own name, probably emanating from the lands under her personal control.

At other times, we know about the influence of European queens because nobles resented that influence. Fastrada (c.764–94), the third wife of Charlemagne, was considered too influential. Extant sources suggest that she could sway her ageing husband to advantage her family and friends; her influence provoked two revolts. In the next generation, Judith, the second wife of Charlemagne's son Louis the Pious, receives perhaps too much blame for instigating the civil war that led to the break-up of the Carolingian Empire. When her son was born in 823, his existence upset the careful inheritance scheme Louis had erected for his three sons by his first marriage. Judith strove relentlessly to win her child a share of the empire, and also persuaded the emperor to favour her own aristocratic family – after all, Judith's kin had married her to Louis for just that purpose. When a complex civil war broke out between Louis and his sons, the venomous attacks on Judith reveal best

OPPOSITE: A modern stained-glass window in Worms Cathedral, Germany, depicting the marriage of Charlemagne and his third wife, Fastrada.

BELOW: In this famous mosaic from the Church of San Vitale, Ravenna, Empress Theodora is depicted carrying her offering to the altar; her husband Justinian approaches the altar in a mosaic on the opposite wall.

how important she was at court. Her enemies accused her of adultery and incest, and succeeded for a time in consigning her to a convent. Judith's son did, however, eventually gain a share of the empire, becoming King Charles the Bald of the territory that came to be known as France. Fear of queens' influence explains the ninth-century custom in Wessex that made them 'king's wives' rather than queens and forbade them to sit beside the king on the royal throne.

Other queens in Europe came to the fore when embattled kings could not trust anyone else. One such woman was Angelberga, who married the future emperor Louis II in c.851. She played an active role in government as a negotiator and viceroy in parts of Italy. Angelberga also conducted military campaigns and is cited in sources as a judge. Her final act was to convene the council to decide the succession when Louis died in 875 without a son.

Similarly, the insecure kings of tenth-century France sometimes relied heavily on their wives. Queen Emma led the military defence of Laon in 927 as well as several other military engagements. Gerberga also led Laon's

RIGHT: **Heroine or villain? Olga of Kiev was apparently both to the nineteenth-century painter of this icon. A vigorous sponsor of Christianity, Olga exacted a bloody revenge on her husband's murderers. The glaring eyes of this icon and even the way she clutches a cross suggests she is a dangerous woman.**

defence after the Normans captured her king in 948, and she continued to direct campaigns while regent for her son. Most strikingly, the bigamous Cnut the Great controlled more territory after his conquest of England than he had deputies he could trust. He eventually sent his first wife, Aelfgifu of Northumbria, along with her son to serve as viceroy in Norway; his second wife, Emma of Normandy, may have held a similar position when Cnut had to be in Denmark rather than England.

Finally, one of the most famous cases of shared rule is the Byzantine imperial couple Justinian and Theodora. Theodora (c.490–548), originally a circus performer and prostitute, married the heir to the throne and the two were inseparable until her death in 548. Some of Justinian's laws specifically state that he received advice from Theodora; she might have been especially involved in statutes giving women greater legal rights. Her fingerprints are also visible in religious issues; her support of monophysitism (doctrine that Christ had one nature, both divine and human) made her a saint of the Syrian Orthodox Church. The historian Procopius says that she and Justinian did everything together, and certainly Justinian's reign lost steam following Theodora's death.

The next empress, Sophia, wife of Justin II, received public recognition for her role in power. Sophia was unwilling to relinquish authority when her husband died in 578 and plotted to assassinate his successor, although she failed and suffered the confiscation of all her property.

BAD WOMEN?

As in the ancient world, when women ruled, the modalities of power were basically the same as for men, including such autocratic methods as frequent killing and vigorous suppression of enemies. In a number of cases, women rulers who have been labelled as violent or even vicious were only acting as any male would have done. For example, no account of Olga of Kiev, regent for her son 945–64, is complete without telling how she hunted down the men who had assassinated her husband Igor I and had them boiled to death, as if this revenge were something extraordinary. If her son had been of age, he would doubtless have done the same. Wu Zetian took lovers, including two brothers in their twenties whose affair with the empress began when she was 72 – a situation that would hardly raise an eyebrow in a male ruler.

Even the murderous feud between the Merovingian queens Brunhild and Fredegund is by no means exceptional in the history of that bloodthirsty dynasty, except that the protagonists were women. Fredegund instigated the quarrel by convincing her lover Chilperic I to murder his wife – Brunhild's sister – and marry her instead. Brunhild vowed revenge and both did their

OVERLEAF: **In a brazen display, Frankish Queen Fredegund visited Bishop Praetextatus, who had been mortally wounded by her own assassins. The historian Gregory of Tours tells that the bishop cursed the queen, a scene captured by Lawrence Alma-Tadema in this painting.**

best to kill friends, supporters and relatives of the other. Fredegund was responsible for the death of a number of stepsons and at least one bishop. These life stories express hard truths about early medieval queens. They were powerful in the sense of having henchmen willing to carry out their commands, but were relatively powerless in that their authority was almost always dependent on the favour of a royal man.

THE WITCH QUEEN

ABOVE: A coin depicting King Kshemagupta and Queen Didda of Kashmir.

Perhaps the most notorious queen of the early Middle Ages was Didda of Kashmir (c.924–1003), who ruled in the second half of the tenth century. Didda had an independent power base as heiress of Lohara, which united with Kashmir upon her marriage. Her royal birth probably eased her path as regent for her son and then grandsons between 958 and 980.

Didda ruled vigorously, suppressing several rebellions and taking bloody revenge on her enemies and their families. Then, in 980, she arranged for her youngest grandson to be tortured to death (after previously murdering his brother) in order to rule independently, with her lover as prime minister.

Or did she? Most of what we know about Didda comes from a source that was written in the twelfth century, long after her death. Kashmir was one of the few regions of India in which female rule was even possible, and the author may have purposefully painted as dark a picture of Didda as possible, being biased against the notion of a woman ruling at all.

This odd dynamic of powerful powerlessness had a particularly great impact on the Byzantine Theophano (c.955–91). Her first husband, Romanos II, died suddenly in 963. Despite having just given birth, the empress was able to act quickly, claiming the regency for her sons Basil and Constantine. Nonetheless, a general, Nikephoros II Phokas, seized the throne in a coup after only a few months. Theophano agreed to marry him, probably as the best chance to preserve the throne for her children. They did not get along; she likely hated him from the start. In 969, Theophano joined with her lover to assassinate Nikephoros, planning to raise the lover to the purple in his stead. Once he had gained power, however, John Tzimisces exiled the woman to whom he owed the throne.

Other royal women killed those who stood between them and power. Aelfthryth of England reputedly had her stepson Edward 'the Martyr' assassinated in 978 so that her own son could inherit (with herself as regent). Drahomira of Bohemia, forced to share the regency for her son Duke Wenceslas with her mother-in-law, hired assassins to murder the older woman in 921. Or was it simply lust for power? Wenceslas' grandmother Ludmila was a strong patron of Christianity, which was just taking root in Bohemia at the time. The murder could as easily be read as desperate protection of Drahomira's ancestral religion than as a power grab. Ludmila's advocates won the war of words. Ludmila was acclaimed as a saint, and pious legend assured that the only story we know is of a godly woman trying to do her best for her grandson, slaughtered at the whim of a designing female.

LEFT: Ludmila of Bohemia was credited with raising her grandson, later canonized as St. Wenceslas, as a pious Christian. The two are shown devoutly praying at a Mass in this 1837 illustration.

La royne dangleterre
qui desiroit a des
fendre son pais
que le mandement des
glois se faisoit a neuf
teau se trayzent celle

FEMALE SOVEREIGNTY IN THE HIGH MIDDLE AGES

Sitt al-Mulk was the older sister of the Fatimid caliph al-Hakim, ruler of an extensive empire based in Egypt in the early eleventh century. After years of al-Hakim's unbalanced behaviour and oppression, Sitt al-Mulk probably joined the conspiracy that arranged the caliph's disappearance in 1020 (his body may have been dismembered and smuggled away under the guards' cloaks). Sitt al-Mulk then ruled the caliphate for four years as regent for her young nephew. In that time, she restored stability and won her people's deep affection. She held public power despite deeply entrenched beliefs that governance was a job for men. In a second example, Queen Dowager Chonghui of the Choson Dynasty in the mid-fifteenth century initially refused to serve as regent for her grandson; after all, the Korean dynasty had no history of female regency. She only relented when government officials formally requested her to take on the role.

OPPOSITE: **With her husband Edward III campaigning in France, it was left to Queen Philippa of England to rally the Northumbrians to repel a Scottish invasion. In this miniature from the** *Grandes Chroniques de France* **(c.1470), Philippa is shown encouraging her troops before the Battle of Neville's Cross.**

RIGHT: **To highlight her role as ruler rather than consort, on this gold franc, Queen Giovanna I of Naples had herself portrayed as a male king in armour with a sword and sceptre in her hands.**

Both regencies demonstrate how, in the high Middle Ages as before, blood counted for more than customary gender stereotypes. Although in many regions bureaucracies were becoming ever more powerful and managed much of the work of rule, monarchy worldwide remained personal and hereditary. Personal rule made it inevitable that the women of royal houses – both wives and females of royal blood– would play a role, sometimes an immense one, in the functioning of their state. Queens, queen-mothers and sometimes queen-grandmothers either embraced power when opportunity arose or had it thrust upon them. The period from 1000 to c.1450 saw its fair share of women who influenced their husbands and sons, and also of women who enjoyed public

RIGHT: The Fatimid caliph al-Hakim, whose sister Sitt al-Mulk took control of Egypt's government after al-Hakim disappeared in 1020.

power as regents. However, the period also witnessed a surprising number of sovereign women – women who inherited their thrones and were often crowned as 'kings' in recognition that they were rulers in their own name rather than consorts.

These female kings had to find a way to navigate the masculine world of political life. Almost everywhere, women were regarded as incapable or less capable of rule, despite frequent evidence to the contrary. In some lands, when women inherited they had to carefully manoeuvre through cultural norms that forbade their interaction with men who were not their close relatives. Women were rarely educated to rule, since typically they only ascended the throne after years of failed efforts to produce a male heir, or if the death of a brother created a vacancy. Then there was the marriage conundrum. Marriage and childbirth were essential for the continuity of a dynasty, but if society insisted on the subordination of wives to their husbands, did husbands automatically become king and take charge, despite not bearing royal blood themselves? The struggle to resolve such questions is a central theme in the history of royal women during this period.

CONSORT: SOMEONE WHO SHARES THE WORK OF GOVERNMENT

Sometimes the power or influence of a queen is known to us through a single major event that suggests a broader pattern. When the Mongol Hulägu Khan sacked Baghdad in 1258, his wife, a Nestorian Christian princess named Doquz-khatun (d.1265), convinced him to spare all Christians in the city.

LEFT: This fourteenth-century illustration of Rashid al Din's chronicle shows the Mongol siege of Baghdad in 1258.

BELOW: **Khan and Doquz-khatun, portrayed as a new Constantine and Helena in a Syriac Bible of the thirteenth century.**

Philippa of Hainault interceded 58 times in the reign of her husband Edward III of England.

Apart from that monumental act, evidence is slim, but Doquz-khatun appears to have inspired Hulägu to favour Christians throughout the Mongol Empire. By contrast, Queen Zaynab al-Nafzawiyya (d. 1072) played a more general role after she married Yusuf ibn Tashfin, the founder of the Almoravid Empire, in c.1071. Zaynab, a merchant's daughter, moved from concubine to wife. Extant sources describe her as determined and intelligent with a good head for business. She advised her husband at a key moment when he was defending his independence against his former overlord. The best evidence we have of Zaynab's importance, however, is that some contemporaries described her as a sorceress, suggesting that they regarded her influence over her husband as excessive.

ABOVE: **The chronicler Froissart tells that when Calais surrendered to Edward III of England he demanded that the leading citizens surrender themselves to be hanged. They were only spared when Queen Philippa begged her husband for their lives. Sculptor Auguste Rodin has caught the moment of pardon in his famous sculpture group 'The Burghers of Calais,' with some still despairing even as others realize they have been saved.**

As in the early Middle Ages, European documents can reveal the influence of queens when they appear either as witnesses or interceding for favours or offices. For example, Philippa of Hainault formally interceded 58 times in the reign of her husband Edward III of England. By the later Middle Ages, reginal intercession had become so organized in that kingdom that queens received one-tenth of any gifts made to kings. Nor was the sway of queens over their husbands limited to Europe or to monogamous societies. In India's Delhi Sultanate (1206–1526), for instance, members of the harem were deeply involved in political life, and many queens had access to great authority. Such influence might of course backfire, if a queen's 'interference' disturbed too many vested interests. An extreme example is the death of Queen Gertrudis of Hungary in 1213, assassinated by noble rebels who blamed the queen and her foreign relatives for their lost clout at court.

WOMEN EMPOWERED BY ABSENT MEN

A number of factors could lead to a queen exercising public power during the reign of a husband or son. The most obvious situation creating the need for the queen to serve as viceroy was the absence of the king. For example, Eleanor of Aquitaine (c.1122–1204), although never formally regent, secured the oaths of England's nobility for her son Richard since he was not on the

Queens issued commands visibly and publicly in the king's absence. In an age of poor roads and slow communications, having somebody with authority on the spot was vital.

OPPOSITE: **Katharine Hepburn as Queen Eleanor of Aquitaine in *The Lion in Winter* (1968), portraying a dominating figure even though she had been imprisoned for years by her husband, the ageing Henry II.**

island when his father died. She later played a crucial role raising money for Richard's ransom after he was captured while returning from the Third Crusade. Crusades led many women to take on administrative tasks they might not have enjoyed otherwise, and queens were no exception. Eleanor, while still queen of France, went on the Second Crusade herself, but several queens stayed home as viceroys for their crusading husbands. When Philip II of France went east, he named his mother Adela of Champagne as regent and guardian of his son in his absence. The redoubtable Blanche of Castile similarly ruled 12th-century France when her son Louis IX set out on the first of his two crusades, formally reclaiming the power she had probably never completely laid down when her son reached adulthood.

Queens issued commands visibly and publicly in the king's absence. In an age of poor roads and slow communications, having somebody with recognized authority on the spot was vital. The Byzantine emperor Alexios I Komnenos was fortunate in his eminently capable mother, Anna Dalassena (c.1025–1102), who had in fact helped engineer the coup that raised him to the purple. She was regent during the campaigns of Alexios' early reign, entrusted with control of the entire civil administration, although she was never empress herself. It was Anna, even more than her son, who restored stability to the empire after the crises of the 1070s, as she revived the imperial administration and reformed administration within the royal palaces. Even more vitally, Stephen of England's queen – confusingly named Matilda like his cousin and rival for the throne – commanded the counteroffensive after he was captured in a civil war in 1141.

The problem of absenteeism was exacerbated when a ruler held several territories and could not be in two places at once. When William conquered England in 1066, the now-queen Matilda was his preferred viceroy in Normandy, one of the few people he could completely trust with authority enough for the job. Monarchic pluralism became more common in Europe in the late Middle Ages, and rulers turned to female members of their family for help, a process that reached its height in the Spanish Empire of the sixteenth century. However, much earlier, in the fourteenth century, Elizabeth Piast was pressed into service by her son Louis I, who ruled both Hungary and Poland and needed a resident regent for the latter; Elizabeth held the post from 1370

ABOVE: In this rather comic 1932 sketch, the cousins Matilda and Stephen are depicted fighting it out for the crown of England in the English Civil War of 1135–54.

to 1380. Most striking was the situation of Maria of Castile (1401–58), queen to Alfonso V of Aragón. The couple lived together for the first 11 years of their marriage, but when Alfonso conquered the kingdom of Naples he spent most of the rest of his life there. Maria remained ruler of Aragón for more than 20 years, invested with the office 'queen-lieutenant.'

Outside of Europe, a similar situation is mostly seen in the far-flung Mongol Empire, where women exercised more power for a longer period over a wider area than anywhere else. The Muslim traveller Ibn Battuta was shocked to find joint rule among the Mongols. Chinggis (Genghis) Khan invested his four daughters with strategically important sub-kingdoms, apparently considering them more competent than their brothers. Other khans gave formal power to kinswomen.

Notably, Absh Khatun, daughter-in-law of Hulägu Khan, refused to remarry when her husband died. Hulägu sent her to rule Persia, which she did very capably from 1263 to 1287. Mongol women could also wield conditional power effectively. Thus, although Töregene Khatun was never officially proclaimed as a ruler, as the powerful wife of Ögedei Khan she was in a position to take charge of the entire Mongol Empire when her husband died in 1241. There could be no new great khan until Mongol forces throughout Eurasia had pulled back from their conquests for a new election. Töregene therefore ruled for five years, supervising further conquests and eventually engineering the election of her eldest son as the new great khan.

A king's incapacitation could thrust a queen into power whether she wanted it or not, sometimes forcing her into desperate measures to preserve the dynasty and her own children's rights. Such was the case with Isabeau of Bavaria (1371–1435), wife of Charles VI of France, and with Margaret of Anjou (1430–82), who married Henry VI of England. Both women had very difficult lives and fought stubbornly for their families with every tool available to them when their husbands plunged into mental illness. Isabeau was formally designated by edict as Charles VI's representative during his periods of mental breakdown. She had to negotiate the minefield of the king's overly powerful and antagonistic relatives, the renewal of the Hundred Years

War and her own son's efforts to oust her from power. Isabeau responded vigorously, and the fact that her son imprisoned her in 1417 (she was soon rescued by an ally) perhaps helps explain why she formally declared the young man to be a bastard in the Treaty of Troyes that made Henry V of England heir to the French throne. Queen Margaret, by contrast, fought consistently for the rights of her son, as rival claimants to the throne twice

WORKING WITH THE MONGOL KHANS

LEFT: The imposing yurt of Töregene Khatun, regent of the Mongol Empire for five years, was the backdrop for the inauguration of her son Guyük as great khan.

The king of Kirman, a province in Persia, was a vassal of the great khan. When he died in 1257, leaving only young children, the khan was content to give his widow Kutlugh Turkan (c.1208/1213–83) sovereign power. Kutlugh ruled for 26 years, a golden age for Kirman thanks to her deep concern for her people's welfare. She founded public granaries and constructed mosques as well as charitable institutions. After decades of success, however, a new khan displaced her in favour of her stepson. Kutlugh protested without success, but her daughter Padisha Khatun was able to replicate her mother's independence.

Padisha, who had been raised as a boy in order to evade Mongol overlords' policy of forcibly marrying heiresses to members of

their own royal house, was eventually found out and wed to Hulägu's son, Abaka Khan. Padisha convinced him to give her Kirman. She ruled for four years, calling herself 'sovereign of the world' on her gold coins. Eventually, however, Padisha Khatun fell prey to the power politics of the time; she was murdered in 1295.

That Kutlugh and Padisha were able to claim Kirman at all demonstrates Mongol acceptance that ruling women could be as competent as men. Another example is Sorghaghtani (d. 1252), the mother of both Möngke and Khubilai Khan. Married to a member of the Mongol royal family, Sorghaghtani was widowed and then convinced the khan to give her rule of a province of northern China. Sorghaghtani proved to be an enlightened ruler, promoting both religious and cultural tolerance with her employment of Chinese advisers. Möngke's political acumen allowed her to become great khan and after her death, her younger son Khubilai also ruled.

ABOVE: **A miniature from Christine de Pisan's *Book of the City of Ladies*. In this scene, the author presents her book to the French queen, Isabeau of Bavaria. As was the norm, the queen's attendants were female, and she receives the author in the privacy of her bedchamber.**

deposed and then murdered her incapacitated husband in England's Wars of the Roses. Margaret raised the army that defeated and killed Richard of York after he claimed the throne. She only gave up the fight after the death of both husband and son left her with no further legal claim to the English throne. Both women were willing to fight fire with fire, at times shocking their contemporaries, who expected more delicacy from women. Later, Shakespeare described Margaret as a 'tiger's heart wrapped in a woman's hide.' Isabeau's critics were more vitriolic, accusing her of adultery, incest, treason, greed and neglect of her own children.

Notably, some consorts were strong enough in their own right to resist an unreasonable spouse. Two examples from different parts of the world illustrate this point. Empress Kassi (b. 1241) of Mali was a member of an important noble clan. When her husband divorced her in order to marry a commoner, the court noblewomen sided with Kassi and refused to recognize her successor. Kassi then convinced her cousins to rebel. Although the rebellion was eventually defeated and Kassi convicted of treason and exiled, her story demonstrates the depth of her political networks and the wellspring of public sentiment on which some consorts could rely. The second rebellion against an unsatisfactory husband occurred in fourteenth-century England. King

Edward II had married the French princess Isabella (c.1295–1358), only to slight and insult her, preferring the company of his male lovers. However, after alienating support in the country, he found he needed Isabella's connection to France. He sent her on a diplomatic mission to her brother, but once in France, Isabella made common cause with nobles Edward had exiled. They invaded England, where they deposed and soon murdered the king. Isabella and her lover then ruled for several years for the adolescent Edward III, until he succeeded in seizing personal power in a coup.

MOTHER POWER

As Isabella's regency proves, rule for minors continued in this period as the least-contested route to power for women, thanks to mothers' role as protectors of their children. Even in regions where orthodox thought absolutely denied women a political role, mothers became regents. In China's Song Dynasty, no fewer than nine dowagers held power, although their role was strictly limited to cater to notions of 'propriety.' It became a formal rule that when meeting with officials the female regent should remain hidden behind a curtained divide. Empress regents were also forbidden from holding court in the great audience hall, a prerogative reserved for emperors. Beneath this veneer of female modesty, however, such women could exercise real power. Two exceptional examples are Dowager Empresses Liu (969–1033) and Gao (1032–93). Liu rose from humble origins as a court entertainer who caught the heir apparent's eye; he remained loyal to Liu, naming her empress after his first empress died and Liu was already 43 years old. When the emperor died in 1022, Liu became regent for his son by a concubine, and ruled until her death 11 years later. Even more noteworthy was Gao, who became regent for a nine-year-old emperor in 1085. Gao introduced a series of reforms and carefully relied on trusted officials rather than advancing members of her own family. She ruled until

BELOW: Copied from a manuscript produced in c.1445, John Talbot, earl of Shrewsbury, presents his *Book of Romances* to Queen Margaret of Anjou, as King Henry VI looks on.

her death eight years later; contemporaries praised Gao as 'a Yao and Shun among women.' Unusually, Yelü Pusuwan (r. 1163–77), regent of the Western Liao for her nephew, was married and was able to employ her husband as her chief military commander.

The Muslim Ayyubid dynasty also afforded at least one opportunity for a female regent to exercise real power despite restrictive ideas about women's proper place. Dayfa Khatun (d. 1242) ruled the northern Ayyubid state of Aleppo from 1236 to 1242. She played no public role during the minority of her son al-Aziz, but when he died, leaving a seven-year-old son, Dayfa stepped forward to run the governing council. It probably helped that Dayfa was already 52 years old in 1236, but she still carefully maintained propriety; the council would reach a decision, then send their eunuch member to Dayfa in the harem to solicit her opinion and ask permission, before proceeding.

During her regency, Dayfa had to defend her grandson's interests against her own brother al-Kamil, the ruler of Egypt, when she organized a political-military alliance against him. Al-Kamil still invaded, but Aleppo was saved by his death in 1238. Dayfa also arranged the military resistance that fought off the Khwarazmians. Dayfa's strength stemmed from the fact that she was herself a member of the Ayyubid dynasty (having married a cousin), and because the last two decades of Ayyubid rule were marred by crisis and civil war. Similarly benefitting from royal blood, Fatima ruled as regent of the Emirate of Granada in Spain for two successive grandsons between 1325 and 1354. Being of Nasrid blood herself, Fatima commanded the obedience of Granada's subjects.

In Christian lands, too, widows served as regents, with varying degrees of success. Anne of Kiev, queen of France, was replaced as guardian for her son Philip I before he came of age, probably because she remarried. The fear of a second husband's power also influenced the Byzantine emperor Constantine X Doukas. On his deathbed in 1067, he named his wife Eudokia Makrembolitissa regent (1067–71), but demanded her written oath not to remarry or to bring her own relatives into government – clearly trusting a woman on her own more than a woman who was the pawn of court factions. Eudokia, in the perilous military situation of the time, remarried anyway, choosing a general who was then proclaimed emperor.

More humiliating was Agnes of Poitou's ignominious ejection from regency over the German Empire for her son Henry IV. After several years of successful rule, the regency was literally stolen from her when Archbishop Anno of Cologne kidnapped the young king in 1062. Without the person of the king, Agnes had no conduit to claim power; she gave up the fight and retired to Italy. Worst of all, however, was the disastrous end to the regency of Maria of Antioch, who ruled for her son the Byzantine Alexios II. As a

BELOW: Dayfa Khatun was responsible for the construction of the impressive al-Firdaws mosque and *madrasa* (school) in Aleppo. This photograph shows the courtyard of the *madrasa*.

Anton von Werner's graphic painting (1868) shows the infamous 'Coup of Kaiserswerth,' when Archbishop Anno of Cologne kidnapped the young Henry IV of Germany. The boy leaped from the ship in an escape attempt, but the archbishop's men took him from the water.

'Latin' foreigner, Maria was unpopular during a time of intensive east-west tensions, and lacked a family network that might have supported her. The late emperor's cousin Andronikos led an opposition movement against her, eventually orchestrating a massacre of Westerners in Constantinople in April 1182. Wresting effective control of the government from Maria, the next year, he rigged the dowager's conviction for treason. She was imprisoned and strangled with her son being murdered shortly after.

Several Christian regents are noted for their political astuteness. Yolande of Aragón was regent for her son and one of the major political operators of the late Hundred Years War, especially as adviser to her son-in-law Charles VII of France. Three women particularly stand out, however. The first is Adalisa, regent of Sicily for her son Roger II (1101–12). She handled a volatile situation – the Normans had only recently conquered the island and both Muslim and Greek rebellions were a constant threat, not to mention overly independent Norman lords – with skill. When Roger grew up, instead of contending for power with her own son, Adalisa embraced a new opportunity: King Baldwin I of Jerusalem asked for her hand in marriage. Baldwin clearly wanted the wealth of the widow, probably past childbearing years; she for her part was doubtless motivated by desire to serve the holy city of Jerusalem. However, she also won an agreement that, if the couple failed to have a child, the crusader state would go to her son Roger. The agreement ultimately backfired on Adalisa. Since Baldwin had consigned his previous wife to a convent, he technically committed bigamy by wedding the Sicilian. When he fell ill, the patriarch convinced Baldwin to atone by repudiating the match, so he sent Adalisa home – without her dowry.

Blanche of Castile (1188–1252), by contrast, was never outwitted by crafty or greedy men. She displayed her administrative skills at a young age when her husband, the future Louis VIII of France, invaded England in the 1210s: Blanche organized two fleets and an army to support him. Louis died young in 1226, leaving the throne to Louis IX, who was only 12. Blanche faced opposition from nobles who did not want to be ruled by a foreign woman and who more generally opposed the growing power of the French monarchy; they formed a league to seize the regency. Blanche, however, proved strong, raising and leading an army against the rebels. She also had to fight off an English attack in 1230. Her regency ushered in a period of peace and prosperity and her influence over Louis IX remained so strong that at least one modern historian has argued that she should be regarded as a king of France. She served as regent again from 1248 to 1252, while Louis was on crusade.

Most extraordinary of all was Margaret of Denmark, Norway and Sweden (1353–1412). A Danish princess who married the king of Norway, she

OPPOSITE: **This thirteenth-century miniature shows the French queen Blanche of Castile ruling side by side with her young son, Louis IX. Her position with arms raised suggests that she is advising or teaching the youthful king.**

Even when women inherited, men did their utmost to retain the reins of power in their own hands.

became regent of Denmark for her young son in 1375 when her father died. In 1380, her husband also died and she assumed rule of Norway for her son. Margaret lost all legal claim to rule Denmark in 1386 when the son died and a nephew immediately claimed the throne, but clearly the regent had made a good impression on Scandinavia's nobles. They elected the dowager 'Almighty lady and husband and guardian for the whole kingdom of Denmark', the term 'husband' in this sense describing a person in charge of governing the household. In other words, she was permanent regent, and the nobles of Norway soon copied the Danish decision. After Margaret joined the nobles of Sweden in an uprising against their unpopular king, she was proclaimed queen of Sweden in 1388, with the power to name her successor. In 1397, Margaret united the Scandinavian countries with the Union of Kalmar, and ruled the whole union until her death in 1412.

THE HEIRESSES

Most lands accepted that, for the sake of dynastic continuity, a woman could hold the throne in her own name if there were no male heir. An exception was France, where jurists in the fourteenth and early fifteenth century gradually made it self-evident that the throne of France could pass only to and through the male line. They had excluded Princess Jeanne from succession in 1317, mostly because of her dubious paternity, and an assembly barred Philip IV's daughter Isabella from the succession in 1328 – probably because she had just played a role in deposing her husband Edward II of England and was ruling England scandalously with her lover Roger Mortimer. It took considerable searching through old lawbooks to justify the decision, however. Legal grounds were finally found in the Law of the Salian Franks from c.500. A clause of Salic law was interpreted to argue that women were ineligible for the French crown.

Elsewhere, women could inherit – but could they actually rule? Christine de Pisan argued vigorously in her *Book of the City of Ladies* (1405) that they could, but hers was a rare voice against cultural assumptions and the tyranny of Aristotle's views about female incapacity. Even when women inherited, men did their utmost to retain the reins of power in their own hands. A classic case of inheritance with no authority to rule is the 'reign' of Petronilla of Aragón (1137–64). To end an inheritance crisis, Petronilla's father Ramiro

KÖNIGIN MARGRETA

A CASE OF REAL PARTNERSHIP

ABOVE: **Queen Tamar of Georgia with her husband David Sosland. Fresco from the Church of the Dormition in Vardzia.**

One of the most extraordinary woman rulers of the high Middle Ages was Tamar of Georgia (r. 1184–1213). Georgia differed starkly from other Christian lands in its positive attitude towards female power, partly because Christianity itself reached Georgia through a woman, St. Nino. Even the Georgian language helped: Tamar's title of *mepe* – while usually translated as 'king' – is in fact gender neutral, simply meaning a person with sovereign power. There is a totally different Georgian word for a queen consort. This meant that when Tamar's father had her crowned as co-ruler in c.1178, there were no voices to complain that the role was inappropriate for a queen.

The period of co-rule with her father gave Tamar six years to learn how to govern, although she still faced the imperative to marry and bear children to continue the dynasty. Her first marriage, to Prince Yuri, was a diplomatic match and did lead to her husband being declared *mepe*, but Tamar also remained in place as ruler. The couple did not get along, in part because Yuri expected more power. She divorced him on the grounds of drunkenness and sodomy, but Yuri tried twice to depose her, aided by several Georgian nobles. Tamar chose her second husband, her cousin David Sosland. They shared peacefully in rule until David's death in 1207. David's primary role was as military commander, whereas Tamar ran the administration, neatly avoiding the perennial problem that women were considered unable to lead troops in battle. When David died, Tamar had their son crowned as co-ruler, and appears to have gradually shifted the entirety of rule to him.

had left monastic life long enough to beget an heir. He then betrothed the infant to Berenguer IV of Barcelona, who ruled for Petronilla as regent, then as king when she reached marriageable age. Often, women, at least according to extant sources, did little but transmit the royal bloodline. For example, 10-year-old Jadwiga of Poland was elected and crowned as ruling king

ABOVE: **Philip IV of France (centre) and his children, Louis X, Philip V, Charles IV and Isabella of France (right), married to Edward II of England.**

of Poland in 1384, but in 1386 her marriage to Jagiello of Lithuania gave him direct control over her lands. It is unclear if Jadwiga played a political role at all in the few years before she died from complications of childbirth, although her great interest in the conversion of Lithuania to Christianity led a Polish pope to canonize her in 1997. Such transfer of authority to a man via marriage could be violent. When the child Maria inherited Sicily in 1377, her uncle the king of Aragón had her kidnapped. He held Maria for 14 years and then married her to an Aragónese prince half her age – all so Aragón could control Sicily. In a similar situation, Sati Beg ruled Persia in 1338–39, apparently doing well, but was soon deposed and forcibly married to her successor.

Sometimes contemporaries simply assumed that marriage to an heiress conferred the reality of political power. This was usually the case in the Byzantine Empire with dowager empresses who remarried. The eleventh century also saw two Byzantine heiresses, however. The first to occupy the throne, Zoë Porphyrogenita (c.978–1050), came to rule in middle age and promptly married, although when her first husband neglected her, she arranged his murder. However, their disagreement had been over him taking a mistress, rather than his control of government; Zoë passed royal authority over to three successive husbands and an adopted son. The people were loyal to their born-to-the-purple empress, however, as the adoptive son Michael V learnt to his cost when he forced Zoë into a convent. He was eliminated in three days of frenzied rioting, which restored Zoë to the throne along with her sister Theodora, although Zoë soon excluded Theodora from power and instead gave the throne to her last husband. Theodora, who finally inherited in her seventies when Zoë's last husband died, was probably wiser; she never

ABOVE: **Empress Zoë and Constantine IX presenting their gifts to Christ, from a mosaic in Hagia Sophia, Istanbul. To suit Byzantine notions of propriety, Constantine was given the superior position at Jesus' right, despite the fact that Zoë was the heiress.**

married and was thus able to rule in her own name for the 18 months until her death in 1056. Theodora proved to be one of the more successful rulers of the eleventh century, actively making appointments and dispensing justice.

Europe saw several instances where a king took every possible step to assure his daughter's inheritance, only to have his will thwarted after his death. In twelfth-century England, Henry I forced his nobles to swear to uphold the right of his daughter Matilda (1102–67) to the throne, only to have her cousin Stephen seize the prize from under her nose in 1135. Matilda waged an extended civil war to claim her birthright, gaining Normandy but ultimately unable to win rule of England. That this first English civil war lasted for over a decade shows that many in England believed Matilda to be their lawful ruler and were willing to support her in battle. Although Matilda finally gave up the fight, her son succeeded Stephen in 1154. Matilda enjoyed the loyal support of an illegitimate brother in her war with Stephen, but other heiresses were not so fortunate. Sancha of León, Beatriz of Portugal and Carlotta of Cyprus were all deposed by bastard brothers. Maria was crowned king of Hungary in 1382 when only 12 years old. Her coronation witnessed a quarrel over who should perform the ceremony: the archbishop of Esztergom, who had the right to crown kings, or the bishop of Veszprém, who traditionally performed the ceremony for queens. The archbishop won. However, Maria had had little more success than Sancha, Beatriz and Carlotta. The majority of Hungarians thought Maria's cousin Charles III of Naples should rule them. When he invaded, Maria renounced the throne, but her redoubtable mother Elizabeth of Bosnia soon arranged Charles' murder and restored Maria. Outraged supporters of King Charles soon captured and imprisoned both queen and dowager. The mother was murdered. Maria was eventually restored to the throne, but her husband Sigismund of Luxembourg did the real ruling.

Women's notions of propriety could also lead them to make way for men, as was the case with Berenguela of Castile. When her father Alfonso VIII died in 1214, Berenguela became regent for her young brother, only to be quickly replaced by nobles. Then her brother died only three years later, making Berenguela queen regnant of Castile. She soon turned rule of Castile over to her son, however, afraid that she would be unable to lead the military. She remained a close adviser to her son until her death, but held no formal office.

CRUSADER WOMEN

In other cases, the relationship between an heiress and her male family members, whether husbands or sons, was much more ambiguous. Nowhere was this truer than in the crusader states of the Near East, where both the principality of Antioch and the kingdom of Jerusalem saw an extraordinary number of female heirs. Here, the situation was complicated by a frequently precarious military situation that called for male field command, but also by

LEFT: **Matilda effectively lost her bid for the English throne because when she had captured her rival Stephen, she appeared too proud and high-handed. This illustration shows the would-be queen repelling Stephen's wife (also named Matilda) as the latter begged for her husband's release.**

OPPOSITE: **Berengaria of Castile (1180–1246) was queen consort of León. After her husband's death, she returned to her native Castile, where she served briefly as queen regnant in 1217.**

the fact that foreigners who lacked local knowledge and political networks were brought from Europe to marry the heiresses. The complexity of this situation is best appreciated in the case of Queen Melisende (1105–61), whose father Baldwin II died in 1131. Baldwin had already arranged his eldest daughter's marriage, convincing Count Fulk of Anjou to give up his territories in France and move to the East. Once Fulk arrived, he rather than Melisende acted as Baldwin's lieutenant. Fulk apparently assumed that he would hold sovereign power rather than sharing it with the heiress, although both were crowned before Baldwin's death. Melisende, however, had local connections and loyalty. A revolt against Fulk seems in large part to have been a protest against excluding her from government, and, although the rebellion failed, Fulk found it expedient to be more careful of his wife's wishes after that.

On Fulk's death, his young son inherited with Melisende as regent. Or perhaps she was acting as a sovereign, anointed queen who had inherited the realm from her father. Again, the situation was ambiguous, because both mother and son were crowned. Eventually, Baldwin III became restive and demanded that his mother cede rule to him, but she refused as, to her mind, she was the lawful ruler. This resulted in war, showing that Melisende had enough support for her claim to make a fight. Baldwin won, but Melisende's sovereignty was at least in part recognized with a settlement that gave her largely independent control of one region.

Melisende's disagreement with Fulk was settled fairly amicably, but other female heirs had a fight on their hands when their husbands tried to exclude them from a public role. We have seen that Tamar of Georgia had to fend off her first husband's attempts to displace her. Urraca of Castile (c.1077–1126) faced a similar situation. When her brother was killed in battle, Alfonso VI named his daughter heir; she ruled Castile from 1109 to 1126. In accordance with her father's wishes, Urraca married Alfonso I of Aragón, but the couple came to loathe each other, especially as she refused to give him authority in her lands. The marriage was eventually annulled, but much of Urraca's reign was spent seeing off invasions by her former husband, who thought he had a right to rule Castile.

Nowhere was the fight for control of government more visible than in the kingdom of Naples, where both Giovanna I (1325–82) and Giovanna II (1371–1435) strenuously defended their rights against husbands. Giovanna I inherited from her grandfather, Robert the Wise, in 1343; Robert had carefully prepared the ground by naming her heir over a decade previously and making his vassals acknowledge her. A joint coronation was planned with her first husband, Prince Andrew of Hungary, but he was murdered before it took place. Giovanna likely had a hand in the plot, fearing a Hungarian

takeover of the kingdom. Louis I of Hungary then invaded, seeking revenge for his brother's death, and Giovanna was exiled for five years before the pope exonerated her. Giovanna did have her second husband crowned but continued to rule herself, as she did through two more marriages. Still, it was a kinsman who eventually toppled Giovanna from power. She named her niece's husband as heir, but then changed her mind. He invaded Naples, able to do so with Roman support because the queen had supported the wrong side in the Great Schism; he defeated and imprisoned Giovanna in 1382. Her supporters remained loyal, however. When they neared the castle where their deposed queen was being held, she was murdered.

Giovanna II, a 41-year-old widow who succeeded her brother in 1414, was more fortunate, at least in the long run. The year after becoming queen, she married the French Jacques de Bourbon, who held Giovanna prisoner and brought in French foreigners to rule with him. The queen made an alliance with her disgruntled nobles, captured Jacques, excluded him from government and sent him back to France, where he became a monk. Giovanna then ruled Naples herself until her death in 1435.

Two further European examples demonstrate that heiresses could rule successfully, confounding gender expectations and performing all regal tasks, even on the battlefield. Matilda of Tuscany (1046–1115), although not officially a queen, was an independent marquesa of northern Italy who played a vital role in the quarrel between German emperor and pope in the eleventh century. Matilda inherited at age seven when her father died; her mother Beatrice ruled as regent until Matilda came of age, and then the two peacefully shared rule until the mother's death in 1076. As sole ruler of Tuscany from 1076 to 1089, Matilda firmly asserted her independence; she simply left her first husband in his German lands and returned by herself to Tuscany. When, late in life, she formed another marriage alliance at the pope's behest, she soon made it plain to the much younger man that the rule of Tuscany was hers, and hers alone. Matilda was the most important ally of the reform papacy, shielding Rome for a decade from attacks by the German Henry IV. Although she did not wield a sword herself, Matilda was commander general of her forces, often present in the field with them.

BELOW: **It is possible that a queen of sunny Naples like Joanna II might have worn fur, as in this nineteenth-century illustration. Fur was after all a symbol of high status. The ruff around her neck, however, is anachronistic.**

Rex rogat Abbatem! Mathildim Supplicat Atr;

ABOVE: Countess Matilda of Tuscany, a key supporter of the papal reform movement of the eleventh century, also played an important role as mediator between the pope and her cousin, Henry IV of Germany. In this miniature, Henry, escorted by Abbot Hugh of Cluny, begs Matilda to help.

The small kingdom of Navarre also produced independent queens, with the active collusion of nobles who did not want the foreign influence a husband would bring. Navarre had been incorporated into France, but separated again in 1328 because they accepted a female heir – Jeanne II (r. 1346–55) – and France would not. The Navarrese insisted that she was sovereign, raising her on a shield as the authentic heir and demanding that she rule jointly with her French husband rather than hand over all power to him. They did in fact govern jointly, but Jeanne proved herself capable, ruling alone after his death for six years until she died during the Black Death.

In the early fifteenth century another queen of Navarre, Bianca, proved an active and effective ruler. After her first husband died, she governed Sicily for five years for her father-in-law. When she became heiress to Navarre in 1420, Bianca managed most government business, since her younger second husband was usually in Castile.

There were still husband problems, however. Bianca's second husband outlived her by 38 years. Since he had been crowned as king of Navarre, he refused to give her heirs any role in government, even though he had no birthright there.

Razia's reign shows that a Muslim woman could rule despite the cultural limitations placed on women over interaction between the sexes. Razia was a rarity, however, in part because the caliphs always denied spiritual validation to women rulers. As we will see in later periods, the event of a woman becoming head of state most likely took place on the fringes of the Islamic world. Yemen saw two women rulers in the high Middle Ages whose public authority was acknowledged by the proclamation of the *khutba* (Friday sermon at the mosque) in their name as sovereigns. Both ruled with their husbands; Malika (queen) Asma (d. 1087) attended council meetings with her face uncovered. Her daughter-in-law Malika 'Arwa (c.1048–1138), who reigned nearly 50 years, served as deputy for her paralyzed husband. 'Arwa was an able military leader, and contemporaries credited her with the strategy that won the Battle of Jabala in 1088.

Nonetheless, when her husband died, the Fatimid caliph refused to recognize 'Arwa as ruler, ordering her to marry and leave the ruling to her spouse. She did marry a cousin, but kept control of Yemen herself until

'MANLY' WOMEN

No European woman ruler in the high Middle Ages dared transcend cultural norms to the point of dressing as a man or actually striking blows in battle, although as we have seen, several were crowned as 'kings' in recognition of their sovereign power. Some received the accolade from male authors that they behaved in a 'manly' fashion or as viragos – man-women – a designation usually intended as a compliment to underline their firmness and resolve. Yet, women could function as rulers in Christian lands, unrestricted in their contact with men and able to appear in public.

The situation was different for Razia Sultan (r. 1236–40), the only queen regnant

LEFT: The Indian television drama *Razia Sultan* began in 2015, starring Pankhuri Awasthy Rode in the title role. The show explores the challenges the sole female ruler of the Delhi Sultanate faced in a man's world.

of Muslim India in the period of the Delhi Sultanate and Mughal Empire. Razia's father had designated her heir in preference to her two half-brothers, although one seized power after their father's death and killed the other. Razia appealed to the people of Delhi and the army for justice; the would-be usurper was seized and killed.

Razia became ruler and adopted the gender-neutral title 'sultan.' Seeing no other way to rule effectively, she unveiled, cut her hair and dressed as a man, even riding astride her horse like a man. She may have been inspired by less circumscribed women in the Hindu regions of India. Later in the century, one of these, Rudramadevi, ruled as female king of Kakatiya in southern India from 1263 to 1289. Rudramadevi married, but her husband played no role in government and she herself cultivated a masculine image, including male garb and the male grammatical form of her name, the better to take an active part in military campaigns.

Razia's reign did not last long; in a noble rebellion, her troops abandoned her and she was killed by a peasant while fleeing. Her overthrow probably had nothing to do with her gender presentation, but later accounts insisted it was because she had transgressed gender norms. Above all, these sources express shock that she allowed a male Ethiopian slave she favoured to physically help her into the saddle.

ABOVE: **The Mausoleum of Shajar al-Durr in Cairo. This extraordinary woman commissioned the building herself. It was probably completed in 1250, some seven years before Shajar al-Durr's death.**

her death in 1138. Her rule was probably only possible because 'Arwa was a member of Yemen's royal dynasty. Women on distant islands could also inherit thrones. Sultana Khadija ruled the Maldives from 1347 to 1379; her husband served as vizier, but she governed in her own name. Tribhuwana Wijayatunggadewi, also a queen regnant, ruled Java from 1328 to 1350, overseeing a massive expansion of the state with great valour and intelligence; she eventually abdicated in favour of her son.

In a final example, the extraordinary career of Shajar al-Durr (d. 1257) illustrates vividly both the possibilities and the pitfalls of rule in Islamic lands. Shajar al-Durr was a slave concubine who became sole wife and most trusted adviser to the penultimate Ayyubid sultan of Egypt. When her husband al-

Salih died at the height of Louis IX's invasion of Egypt, Shajar al-Durr kept the death secret, running the campaign until her husband's son arrived to take command three months later. The new sultan proved to be a drunkard who threatened both his stepmother and the Mamluk military commanders, which led swiftly to his assassination. This was a remarkable tribute to her military and political acumen. However, her independent reign only lasted for three months in 1250. When the caliph heard of her ascension, he sent a message to the Mamluk leaders: if Egypt has no man capable of ruling, he said, he would send one from Baghdad. Shajar al-Durr tried to hold on to the throne, sending a demand that Syria accept her rule, but her envoy was humiliated instead. When Jordan broke free from Egyptian rule, the female sultan accepted defeat and abdicated, marrying a Mamluk commander and elevating him to the sultanate. She still insisted on recognition of her position, however, and when the new sultan took another wife hostile to Shajar al-Durr, the ex-sultan had him murdered. When the other Mamluk commanders discovered what had happened, they had this singular woman beaten to death.

LEFT: A detail of a gold mosaic in a mihrab from the tomb of Shajar al-Durr, Cairo.

RULING WOMEN IN THE AGE OF EXPLORATION

The Castilians made an important change to the game of chess in the late fifteenth century – the queen became the most powerful figure on the board. Not coincidentally, the ruler of Castile at the time was Queen Isabella I. This reassessment of the chess figure suggests that society had finally accepted that queens could be dynamic and forceful rulers. The reality was, of course, more complicated. The history of women rulers in the period c.1480–c.1620 saw greater divergence between the regions of the world than had earlier times. This era saw a hardening of societal attitudes against female rule in much of Asia (although a few women were able to take up public roles there despite the constraints of patriarchy).

OPPOSITE: **'The Madonna of the Catholic Monarchs'** was painted in the 1490s. The panel depicts Isabella of Castile and her husband Ferdinand of Aragón, their children gathered around them, venerating the Virgin and Child.

RIGHT: **Portrait of Archduchess Margaret of Austria, Duchess of Savoy (1480–1530), in widow's dress, by Bernard van Orley.**

In Europe the situation was more complex, as humanist scholars argued both for and against the abilities of women and spread their ideas more widely thanks to the revolutionary new invention, the printing press. All the while, a rising tide of nationalism and the religious partisanship of the Reformation cast emphasis firmly on rule by members of the native dynasty, even if the heir was a woman. This period saw a surprising number of sovereign queens, above all in Europe, and their societies and they themselves struggled to define their position and power. Non-sovereign royal women were also affected in myriad ways by the challenges of their age, although the size of the Ottoman, Mughal and Spanish empires all gave women unprecedented opportunities to exercise power.

ABOVE: A Castilian coin, depicting Isabella and Ferdinand as equal co-rulers. By contrast, Isabella did not appear on the coinage of her husband's realm of Aragón.

THE FEMALE KINGS OF EUROPE AND BEYOND

Isabella I (1451–1504) was named heir to Castile in 1468; she had not been trained to rule as had her brothers, but instead was taught to be a dutiful and virtuous wife. In the following year, she married Ferdinand, heir to the neighbouring kingdom of Aragón, it being unimaginable that a woman could be without a husband. Isabella had to fight for her throne in a long civil war when her claim was contested by her half-brother's daughter. Nevertheless, immediately upon the death of King Enrique in December 1474, Isabella was proclaimed queen in a public ceremony. The royal standard was raised over her, she took up a lance as symbol of her sovereignty and in procession a rider preceded her bearing the sword of justice. Ferdinand, who was in Aragón at the time, was shocked when he received word of how she had usurped what he regarded as 'male privilege.' He should not have been completely surprised, however. The couple's marriage contract had stressed Isabella's sovereignty in her own land, with Ferdinand designated only the role of prince consort. Ferdinand promised 'virtual obedience' to Isabella and made a commitment to live in Castile; the contract also specified that no government appointments would be made without Isabella's consent.

While in Castile, Isabella remained the senior partner in shared rule. She read mountains of documents, to the point that she became the first female monarch to wear spectacles. The couple shared in the conquest of Granada, the last independent Muslim-ruled state on the Iberian Peninsula, between 1482 and 1492. During that period, Isabella spent considerable time with her troops, serving as quartermaster and treasurer of the army, visiting the camps and establishing field hospitals. Isabella and Ferdinand adopted the motto 'To stand as high, as high to stand, Isabella as Ferdinand' (*Tanto monta, monta tanto, Isabel como Fernando*). In 1496, Pope Alexander VI bestowed the title 'the Catholic kings' on the pair.

Gender equality had its limitations. Ferdinand granted his wife no role in the government of his own kingdom of Aragón. Isabella herself may have regarded her own rule as a unique accident; she ensured her three daughters had a good humanist education, but they were not trained to rule, not even the eldest, Isabella, who was heir presumptive for eight years. The girls' education contrasted strongly to that of their brother Juan. When Isabella died, her daughter heir Juana (1479–1555) was manifestly unprepared to rule. Juana 'the Mad' presents us with a historical mystery. She was proclaimed as sovereign in 1504, but her father Ferdinand had the *cortes* (Spanish parliamentary courts) declare her incapable, with himself as regent. He may simply have been trying to seize control of Castile for himself, however; when Juana's husband Philip the Handsome of Burgundy contested the ruling and gained the upper hand, Ferdinand proclaimed Juana sane but a

BELOW: Queen Isabella of Castile takes pride of place in Francisco Pradilla y Ortiz's 1882 'The Capitulation of Granada.' The painting depicts the surrender of the last emir of Granada to the Catholic monarchs.

prisoner. He then hatched a plot with his son-in-law to sideline Juana, until the *cortes* stepped in and deemed her capable of rule. Juana does appear to have had a legitimate mental breakdown when Philip died in 1506, but was it a permanent lapse into insanity? From 1507 until her death in 1555, she was confined in the fortress of Tordesillas – insane, or maybe simply the prisoner of powerful kinsmen who were greedy for her birthright.

LEFT: **Was Juana '*la Loca*' actually insane? She was certainly unbalanced, at least for a time, when her husband Philip of Burgundy died, refusing to allow the burial of his body. The artist Francisco Pradilla y Ortiz strongly suggests her despair in this painting of 1877.**

How much power a queen's husband should hold was a hotly contested issue. There certainly seems to have been a fear that, if given an inch, husbands might take a mile. It was shocking but hardly surprising that ruling women – or their councils or leading citizens – would do their best to limit these men. An interesting example is the case of Mary of Burgundy, who wed the Habsburg archduke Maximilian in 1477. The day after the wedding, the

Mary's sex was no bar to the succession; the
Protestant plot to prevent her accession involved
another woman, Lady Jane Grey, as its puppet.

MARY'S MISGUIDED MARRIAGES

LEFT: A posthumous portrait of Mary Queen of Scots (c.1610),
presenting her as a Catholic martyr, with a crucifix and prayer
book in hand. Her execution is depicted below her right hand.

Mary (1542–87) became queen of Scotland
in 1542 when she was six days old. Henry
VIII made a vigorous attempt to gain her as
a bride for his son and heir Edward, in a war
romantically called the 'Rough Wooing.' The
Scots, anxious not to be absorbed by their
southern neighbour, instead sent their five-
year-old queen to France, where she married
the heir to the throne – consigning Scotland
to absentee rule in the process. The young
French king Francis II died in 1560, however,
and his widow, unable to find another suitable
continental match, was forced to go home to a
land that was in fact foreign to her.

The need for an heir made it necessary
for Queen Mary to wed a second time. Her
choice fell on Henry, Lord Darnley, against
the wishes of all Scottish factions, and who
proved to be a drunken bully. Mary refused
to bestow the crown matrimonial on Darnley,
which would have given him ruling status,
and Darnley responded with attacks on
Mary's supporters, including murdering her
private secretary before her eyes. Mary was
trapped. She might theoretically have gained
an annulment from the pope, but there was
no pretext in canon law for such a course,
which also would have cast doubt on the
legitimacy of her son, the future James VI.

Darnley was murdered in February
1567 – and the queen was implicated in the
plot. Increasing the doubts about her moral
probity, Mary soon took another husband,
the earl of Bothwell, also a suspect in the
murder. He had apparently abducted and
raped the queen to bring her to marriage. The
nobility of Scotland had had enough; they
captured Mary and forced her to abdicate.
Mary escaped her prison and fled to England,
where she spent the rest of her life as the
'guest' of her cousin Elizabeth, until repeated
plots against the English queen led to Mary's
execution in 1587.

Burgundian mints were ordered not to put Maximilian's name on her coins, and he was excluded from that public recognition despite sharing rule until her death in 1482.

A careful prenuptial agreement, like that between Isabella and Ferdinand, was an essential step to limit a husband's ability to take over. Such was the case with Mary I of England (1516–58), who inherited the throne in 1553 upon her brother's death. Mary's sex was no bar to the succession; the Protestant plot to prevent her accession involved another woman, Lady Jane Grey, as its puppet. The difficulty she faced was instead that her father Henry VIII had declared her to be illegitimate, a problem Mary's half-sister Elizabeth I also later encountered. Mary prudently had herself crowned before summoning a Parliament to confirm that her parents' marriage had been valid.

Mary's coronation blended the ceremonies appropriate for a king and for a queen consort. Like a man, she was girded with a sword; unusually, she received two sceptres – the king's traditional symbol of power as well as one with a dove for the queen. Instead of riding a horse, she was carried in a litter during the procession, with her hair worn loose like a bride.

And a bride she soon was. Already 37 years old at her accession, if Mary were to have a child – and so secure England's return to Catholicism as she hoped – she needed a husband promptly. Mary, deeply under the influence of her cousin Emperor Charles V, soon accepted Charles' son Philip as bridegroom. Spaniards were unpopular in England, and Mary's officials insisted on a prenuptial agreement that protected England from undue influence; Parliament even enacted it as law. By this agreement, Mary retained control of all offices of state and crown lands, which in future could only be granted to native Englishmen. All government business was to be conducted in English. If there were no children and Philip survived Mary, he would receive nothing at all; if there was a child, Philip would be regent.

BELOW: The Habsburg dynasty received a major boost when Emperor Maximilian married the heiress Mary of Burgundy, shown in this engraving by Albrecht Dürer.

After the marriage, Philip was never crowned. Clearly exasperated at being sidelined, Philip refused to learn English and went back to Spain in 1555 as it became clear that Mary would not conceive; he only visited England once more, in the following year.

Jeanne III d'Albret (1528–72), who inherited the throne of Navarre in 1555, was Mary's exact contemporary. Jeanne's husband Antoine de Bourbon demanded that he be recognized as king because a husband is of right the lord of his wife. However, the Estates of Béarn responded that Jeanne was 'their true and national lady' and that marriage and royalty followed different rules. After a five-day debate, the assembly finally accepted, on Jeanne's insistence, that Antoine should be co-ruler. Jeanne soon changed her mind about her husband's right to dominate her after she converted to Calvinism at Christmas in 1560 and Antoine remained a staunch Catholic. Jeanne left her husband and returned to Navarre. The crisis might have continued longer, but Antoine was killed in battle in 1562. Jeanne spent the final decade of her life defending Calvinism, her kingdom and her son, the future Henry IV of France.

Two other European sovereign women in this period started in collaboration with husbands. The Venetian noblewoman Caterina Cornaro (1454–1510) was consort of James II of Cyprus, then regent for her son James III; only when he died in 1473 did she rule in her own name. She held power, although ruling from Venice, for 16 years until the Venetian government forced her resignation and took control of the strategic island. However, the exercise of power can be more clearly seen in the example of Anna Jagiellon (1523–96), daughter of Sigismund the Old of Poland. Poland in the sixteenth century had an elective monarchy and in 1575 the nobles elected Anna – along with her fiancé Stephen Báthory, a match hastily arranged for the 52-year-old Anna, apparently to make her a viable candidate for the throne. Anna ruled in Poland while Stephen was mostly occupied with warfare. After Stephen's death in 1586, rather than remaining as sole ruler, the queen orchestrated the election of her nephew, although she continued to exercise political power until her death in 1596.

THE VIRGIN QUEEN

Of European sovereigns, only Elizabeth I (1533–1603) of England did the unthinkable and refused to marry at all. Although she probably never intended to wed, proclaiming that she was married to England, Elizabeth played the universal assumption that she needed a husband to her own political advantage for a quarter of a century. Years were spent in ultimately fruitless negotiations as princes from the Protestant lands, Catholics like her own brother-in-law Philip of Spain and perhaps even the Muscovite tsar Ivan

OPPOSITE: **Jeanne III d'Albret, queen of Navarre. Jeanne was 42 years old when François Clouet painted this portrait, in 1570.**

the Terrible sought her hand. The expectation of so many governments that they could influence English policy through marriage and therefore lordship over the queen gave Elizabeth time and leverage to establish herself and her own policies.

As with Mary, the taint of illegitimacy was more difficult to overcome than gender expectations; after all, Elizabeth's mother, Anne Boleyn, had been accused of adultery and executed. She also came to the throne at a time of great religious confusion, as Elizabeth's father Henry VIII had broken with Rome, her brother Edward VI's government had brought England down a firmly Protestant path and Mary had restored Roman Catholicism. Elizabeth was able to impose a religious settlement, the 'great Anglican compromise' – one with which most English people could live – soon after coming to the throne. Largely thanks to her repeated marriage negotiations, Elizabeth was able to remain at peace with the Catholic world for over a decade, consolidating her own rule of England in the meantime. She continued a policy of delay and prevarication even after her excommunication in 1570, making indecisiveness an effective tool of government. Elizabeth did, however, prove to be a staunch defender of English and Protestant interests, and the latter years of her reign survived a major war with Spain and successfully prosecuted the Nine Years War in Ireland.

Warfare, as other women rulers also found, was the greatest challenge to Elizabeth's ability to command her male subjects' loyalty. In her famous speech at Tilbury, where she had joined her forces expecting an imminent Spanish invasion in 1588, the queen found it necessary both to acknowledge

DA ... EXPECTAT

POTEST NEC VECL...

that it was unnatural for a woman to command and that, as queen, she was more than 'just' a woman. As she proclaimed: 'I know I have the body but of a weak and feeble woman, but I have the heart and stomach of a king, and of a king of England, too.' The commanders of the English fleet, which engaged in several desperate encounters with the Spanish Armada before a great storm brought it to ruin, remained obedient to the queen's rule, perhaps in part because leaders like Francis Drake were of relatively low rank and owed their standing to the monarch. Noble commanders such as the Earl of Essex in the Nine Years War, however, resented being tied to a woman's apron strings, and Essex eventually launched a rebellion against Elizabeth after being recalled for exercising too much independence. The queen's civil administration was probably as successful as it was because of her political partnership with the utterly loyal William Cecil, who ran the daily work of government but did not challenge the queen's pre-eminence.

The tale of sovereign queens in this period is not complete without acknowledging several ruling women in South East Asia in the later sixteenth and early seventeenth centuries. Ratu Kalinyamat, who governed central Java c.1549–79, came to the throne after her brother and husband were assassinated. She commanded naval expeditions against the Portuguese in their base at Malacca in 1550 and 1574. Even more strikingly, the Malay sultanate of Pattani enjoyed a golden age under the rule of four successive queens in the period 1584–1649. These queens, known as the Green Queen, the Blue Queen, the Purple Queen and the Yellow Queen, came to power after a time of severe fighting in which likely all male members of the dynasty had been killed. The Green Queen stabilized the sultanate, acknowledging Siamese overlordship and furthering trade. There is no mention in historical sources of her ever marrying; when she died in 1616, her heir was her 50-year-old sister, who in turn was succeeded by the youngest sister of the family. The last, the Yellow Queen, was the daughter

BELOW: An anonymous Dutch artist created this engraving depicting the procession of the queen of the Malay state of Pattani in 1602.

of her predecessor. She was deposed by the raja of a neighbouring state after a period of conflict.

Sources for sub-Saharan Africa also become more plentiful during this period, revealing information that suggests many African states had long accepted female rulers when conditions were right. Indeed, one of the earliest oral traditions about a woman's political role in Benin indicates that it was only in the modern period that women were excluded from rule. In the later fifteenth century, when Princess Edelayo was about to be crowned ruler, she was prevented by a 'feminine indisposition.' A new law stated that women could no longer be allowed to reign.

Elsewhere in West Africa, women's rule was simply accepted. For example, Aissa Koli ruled the Kanem-Bornu Empire for seven years (either 1497–1504 or 1563–70). She succeeded her father in the belief that all male members of her family had been killed, when in fact a five-year-old half-brother had been taken away to safety. Aissa Koli eventually learnt of his existence and he was crowned in her place when he reached the age of 12, although she continued to act as his adviser.

The most spectacular African queen of this period was Amina (d. 1610), who ruled the Hausa state of Zazzau (present-day Nigeria) in the later sixteenth century. Amina took the throne after her brother died, probably in 1576. Renowned for her military skills before becoming ruler, she devoted her 34-year reign to territorial expansion, personally taking part in military combat in a manner unheard-of in Europe. Her campaigns built Zazzau into a significant empire, which she further strengthened by constructing earthworks around many of her towns. Amina was not exclusively interested in war, however; she also expanded east-west trade through her territories. Legend hints that contemporaries may have regarded Amina's strong political role as transgressive, telling that she took a new lover in every town she visited, and then had the hapless man beheaded the following morning, like an insatiable

ABOVE: **This ivory mask from Benin represents the queen mother Idia, c.1500.**

QUEENS AND THE RENAISSANCE

The Renaissance – that European intellectual movement dedicated to the recovery or 'rebirth' of classical Greek and Roman learning – was in general not kind to women. Although the rediscovery of Plato's writings in the West provided a valuable corrective to Aristotle's profoundly negative views about the female of the species, Plato's arguments for women's abilities were almost drowned out as scholars digested largely negative Greek and Roman stereotypes, viewed through the lens of the hypermasculinity that dogged the period.

Although a queen like Elizabeth I of England might receive an outstanding humanist education that taught her critical thinking skills denied to most women in history, education was not enough to convince many men that a woman was capable of rule. It was rare that scholars such as Cornelius Agrippa argued against the arbitrary power of men. Agrippa devoted his *Female Pre-eminence: or The Dignity and Excellency of that Sex above the Male* of c.1506 to the argument that women are as capable as men and simply need education and opportunity to prove their mettle.

Agrippa was definitely not in tune with the feeling of his times. Far more popular were the views expressed by the Scottish cleric John Knox (pictured) in *The First Blast of the Trumpet against the Monstrous Regiment of Women* ('regiment' in the sense of regimen or rule) in 1558. The work is an extended diatribe against Queen Mary in England, and also against the regents Marie de Guise in Scotland and Catherine de' Medici in France. Knox argued vehemently that women's rule goes against the laws of both God and nature, thus joining the Aristotelian argument of female biological inferiority and the view expressed in Genesis that God made women subject to men. It is important to note, however, that while Knox doubtless believed what he wrote, he was also motivated by the confessional politics of the era. He himself was a staunch Calvinist, whereas the queens he attacked in his treatise were all Roman Catholic. Indeed, the second half of the sixteenth century saw a great outpouring of works critical of women holding power, almost always strongly connected to a female figure who held a different religious affiliation from the author. Knox quickly backpedalled when the Protestant Elizabeth came to England's throne in 1558. She had, however, read the *The First Blast of the Trumpet* , and wanted nothing to do with Knox.

praying mantis. Such accounts, which if true would have been extraordinarily wasteful, suggest that Amina was regarded to some extent as monstrous. Of course, the same could be said of most ruling women in this period, at least in the eyes of some of their male contemporaries.

AN AGE OF POWERFUL REGENTS

Nowhere was it accepted without question that a mother should rule as regent for an underage son after her ruler husband died, but in some places such a regency was more possible than in others. Despite the strong showing of regents earlier in Chinese history, for example, the founder of the Ming Dynasty in 1368 decreed that women should have no role in governance, thus reinforcing cultural attitudes about women's subordination to men. As a result, only one woman served as regent during the entire dynasty, Dowager Empress Zhang (d. 1442), who ruled for a young grandson, and even that was unofficial. In Europe, two examples demonstrate the conditional nature of female regency. In England, when Edward IV died in 1483, Queen Elizabeth Woodville (c.1437–92) was in far too weak a position to claim guardianship for her young son. The daughter of gentry, she had won King Edward through her sexual allure; her newly prominent family was deeply resented by many nobles, including Edward's brother, who claimed the regency for himself and soon deposed (and probably murdered) his young nephew on the grounds that the marriage between Edward and Elizabeth had not been legal.

BELOW: **As shown in this nineteenth-century engraving, after King Edward IV's death his widow, Elizabeth Woodville, felt so threatened that she was forced to seek sanctuary at Westminster Abbey with her children.**

The second example, Margaret Tudor (1489–1541), queen consort of Scotland, did have a royal pedigree as Henry VIII's sister to support her claim to rule for the young James V after her husband was killed in the Battle of Flodden (1513). Initially, the Scots accepted her as regent, despite her being pregnant with another child at the time. However, soon after giving birth, Margaret secretly married Archibald Douglas, Earl of Angus, knowing full well that other Scottish nobles would oppose the match. When it was discovered, the council insisted that by marrying without consent Margaret had terminated her regency – demonstrating a typical view that by remarrying, a woman could no longer be trusted to act in the interests of children of the first marriage. Margaret resisted, naming Angus as co-regent and attempting to remain in power, but the couple were displaced by force in 1515.

One of the most extraordinary regents of the late fifteenth and sixteenth centuries was the Mongol queen Mandukhai the Wise (d. 1510). Working alongside her husband, she reunited the large family of Mongol peoples. The dream of a great Mongol Empire faltered when Mandukhai's husband died, but the dowager rose to the challenge by bringing the last direct descendant of Chinggis (Genghis) Khan – the seven-year-old Dayan Khan – out of hiding and ruling for him. Her overwhelming victory over the Oirat Mongols reunited all Mongols for the first time in a century. Mandukhai continued to govern for the rest of her life, marrying Dayan Khan when he turned 19, probably as a symbolic gesture to assure continuity.

A EUROPEAN AGE OF FEMALE RULE

Most known female regents in this period were in Europe, and the length and vigour of their rule helps reinforce the notion that the sixteenth century was an age of women, at least as far as governance was concerned. In Scotland, Margaret Tudor's regency was short, but her daughter-in-law, Marie de Guise, proved strong if controversial as regent for Mary Queen of Scots. When the infant Mary inherited in 1542, at first James, earl of Arran served as regent. In 1554, however, he was deposed to make way for the queen dowager. Marie naturally favoured French interests – her own daughter, by that time living in France, was being educated to wed the heir to the French throne, which was itself a matter of contention. More importantly, the ruling classes of Scotland decisively turned in favour of Calvinism, whereas Marie's family in

France were staunch defenders of Catholicism. Marie did her best to chart a middle course, advocating religious tolerance, but John Knox's fiery sermons, many directed against the whole principle of female rule, made the Protestant faction ever more strident. When Marie finally took steps to suppress Protestantism, it resulted in a rebellion, which toppled Marie from the regency a year before her death in 1560.

Caterina Sforza (1463–1509), regent of Imola and Forlì after her husband was assassinated in 1488, came to a stickier end. Caterina had proven her strength well before her young son Ottaviano inherited the region. When her husband's uncle, Pope Sixtus IV, died in 1484, Caterina had occupied the Castel

Isabella was a subtle and skilled negotiator; the people of Mantua admired and respected her, and few were eager to have Francesco resume personal rule.

Sant' Angelo in Rome, refusing to hand it over until her husband's title and lands were guaranteed. She increasingly ruled for her sickly husband before his death and then as regent governed well, reducing taxes and keeping her lands out of the warfare that plagued Italy. She was, however, deeply criticized for promiscuity, which gave a particularly rapacious pope a pretext to move against her. Alexander VI declared Caterina to be a 'daughter of iniquity', and granted her lands to his own son, Cesare Borgia. Caterina resisted, commanding her troops personally and declaring 'If I have to lose, although I am a woman, I want to lose in a manly way.' She was captured when Cesare took her fortress of Ravaldino. He allowed his soldiers to rape her repeatedly, then imprisoned her in a dungeon for 18 months until she renounced her rights.

The career of Isabella d'Este, Marquesa of Mantua (1474–1539), was much happier, although it still exposes some of the difficulties a female political operative faced in a man's world. We have more insight into her mind than any other earlier woman ruler thanks to the survival of a massive archive of correspondence – 28,000 letters she received and about 12,000 that she wrote herself. This highly educated woman had every opportunity to shine as a patron of the arts. She was also a political figure, as her husband Francesco Gonzaga was frequently away campaigning. Isbaella's political acumen, considerably greater than Francesco's, gradually led to a rift between them, especially when Isabella ruled Mantua independently in 1509–12 while her husband was held hostage in Venice. Isabella was a subtle and skilled negotiator; the people of Mantua admired and respected her, and few were eager to have Francesco resume personal rule. Repeated quarrels led Isabella to travel extensively until her husband died in 1519 and the marquesa returned to Mantua to rule as regent for her son Federico. One of the most interesting examples of Isabella's political skill and humanity is the role she played in the 1527 sack of Rome. The dowager was visiting Rome at the time, and the presence of her son in the invading army gave her protection. She opened her house as a refuge for some 2,000 people fleeing the violence. When the city had calmed, Isabella successfully negotiated safe passage for all of them.

In France, Salic law did not prevent women from serving as regents, although they could not be sovereigns; bad luck and biological accident

assured several Frenchwomen positions of great power. Probably the most
successful and uncontroversial was Anne of France (1461–1522). Anne's
brother Charles VIII came to the throne in 1483. He was almost 14 years
old, but in poor health and unready to rule. Anne, his elder by eight years,
therefore claimed the regency. Anne's rule was challenged: the duke of Orléans
tried to seize the king and thus the government with the support of the
dowager queen. Orléans demanded a meeting of the States General to depose
Anne, only to have the assembly side with her instead. Unwilling to accept
defeat, Orléans declared war to win what he thought were his rights, a conflict
dubbed the 'Mad War' that was more a reaction against royal centralization
than an attack on Anne personally. Despite international interference, Anne

LEFT: **Isabella d'Este, one of the most striking figures of the Italian Renaissance, appears as a bold beauty in this portrait by Titian, painted in the 1530s.**

A BLOODY END

One of the strongest regents of the sixteenth century was Durgavati, rani of the Hindu kingdom of Gondwana (d.1564). After being widowed in c.1545, Durgavati became regent for her infant son, Vir Narayan. During the 19 years she ruled and then co-ruled her state, the rani fought off repeated foreign threats. However, in 1564, the neighbouring Mughal Empire, under emperor Akbar, launched a massive invasion. Durgavati and her son worked together to counter the attack, leading their troops in the bloody two-day Battle of Narhi. They came close to victory, until the son was wounded and had to be sent to safety; the departure of so many troops to defend him weakened the Gondwana army, leading to defeat. Durgavati herself fought until the bitter end. After being wounded by two arrows, she killed herself to avoid capture by the enemy.

ABOVE: **Madan Mahal Fort, Jabalpur, India. The fortress dates back to the eleventh century, but is especially associated with Rani Durgavati, who died fighting the Mughals.**

emerged triumphant, proving to be shrewd and politically adept. Charles eventually assumed personal rule, but Anne served as regent again when he invaded Italy.

Louise of Savoy (1476–1531) also served as regent of France while a king campaigned in Italy. In this case, however, Louise, mother of Francis I, had never been queen; Francis succeeded when his cousin Louis XII died childless in 1515. Louise was clearly her son's most important adviser in the early part of his reign; he consulted her daily. It was therefore natural that she, rather than his queen, be named regent in the king's absence. Her experience in government became essential when Francis was captured in the Battle of Pavia (1525) – the decisive engagment of the Italian War of 1521–26. It took a year of highly skilled diplomacy to secure the king's release, during which time Louise succeeded in wooing England away from alliance with Spain, weakening the emperor sufficiently to consider releasing his rival. With the cream of the French army captured or destroyed, Louise had to navigate France through the threat of foreign invasion.

OPPOSITE: **Anne of France, who while still a young woman successfully served as regent for her younger brother, Charles VIII, shown here in a nineteenth-century lithograph.**

We witness a similar reliance on a mother in a military situation with Queen Mother Hamida Banu Begum of India's Mughal Empire. In 1589, when Sultan Akbar campaigned in Afghanistan, he had his mother guard Delhi, believing her to be more trustworthy than any man.

THE FORCE OF CATHERINE DE' MEDICI

The most notorious queen mother of French history was Catherine de' Medici (1519–89), three of whose sons became successive kings of France. Her reputation still suffers from the propaganda wars of her lifetime, when she was blamed for attacks on French Protestants and rivals for power attacked her for her inferior birth and foreignness. However one regards her, it is impossible to ignore Catherine's impact on France. The wife of Henry I, she bore him 10 children, but she was still publicly humiliated by the position her husband afforded his mistress.

When Henry was killed in a jousting accident in 1559, Catherine tried to claim the regency for Francis II, but the noble Guise family engineered a coup to snatch control of the government for themselves. Nevertheless, Francis II's official acts began with the affirmation: 'this being the pleasure of the queen, my lady mother.' When Francis died in December 1560, Catherine seized control of the government in a coup. The Estates General duly proclaimed her 'governess of France' for the youthful Charles IX.

Catherine de' Medici was a highly active regent who publicly presented herself as a power figure, which may account for some of the criticism she received. The seal she used for official documents depicted her crowned and bearing a sceptre with the inscription 'by the grace of God queen of France and mother of the king.' During the regency, she surrounded herself with a massive court of 169 female attendants, the most of any queen of France. She also, however, adopted a rather masculine persona for the time, riding astride for her beloved sport of hunting. As regent, Catherine worked for religious compromise and tolerance, even arranging the marriage of her daughter Marguerite to the Huguenot leader Henry of Navarre. Still, tempers ran ever higher, culminating in the St. Bartholomew's Day Massacre of French Huguenots in 1572, for which Catherine received the blame. She continued to exercise a strong influence over her final son to become king, Henry III, until her death in 1589.

THE ONE YOU CAN TRUST

In monarchies, delegating power to women in the family has been common, driving home the truth that rule is a family affair. After all, even in a well-developed bureaucracy, blood ties provide a unique combination of family loyalty and prestige. Especially in larger states, a non-related regional governor appointed by the crown might feel the temptation to claim independence or even try to seize the whole government. To a considerable degree, this difficulty extended to male members of royal families as well, men whose sense of royal entitlement could lead them to regard themselves as equal to the brother or father who actually wore the crown. The safest option was to vest power in a royal woman – a wife, mother, sister or even aunt – whose reputation was bound to the success of the dynasty.

Most queens played a role in the work of government, for example, serving as a conduit for petitions or representing the crown at special events or simply through their self-representation at court. It is usually impossible to know how much actual power they exercised behind the scenes, since royal enactments remained in the name of the king. An exception to this invisibility was Queen Catalina of Portugal (1506–57), who in 1525 married King João

RIGHT: In this painting of the Saint Bartholomew's Day Massacre (24 August 1572), Catherine de' Medici is shown emerging from the Château du Louvre to inspect a heap of bodies.

Charles set the precedent for depending on the Habsburg women, not just as unofficial advisers but also as regents and governors. He simply could not be everywhere at once.

III. João was a procrastinator who was uninterested in government, leaving Catalina to take the lead in ruling Portugal during a period of intensive overseas exploration and expansion. She was the only queen of Portugal ever formally given a place on the privy council, which even met in her own apartments. Nothing was done without Catalina's input, and diplomats openly acknowledged that it was the queen rather than the king who was ruling. When João died in 1557, his heir was a three-year-old grandson, whose mother Juana left to be regent of Spain, leaving Catalina to rule Portugal. Queen Catalina remained in charge until her retirement in 1562, pressured by her husband's brother to finally surrender rule.

The departure of Catalina's daughter-in-law to be regent of Spain was merely one of many instances when women of the Habsburg dynasty were given formal government roles. Juana (1535–73) was Philip II of Spain's youngest sister. She had been widowed in 1554 and, although only 18 years old at the time, was asked to return to Spain to serve as regent while Philip was in England and then the Netherlands. She undertook all state business until Philip's return to Spain in 1559, during which time she became Europe's first and only female Jesuit, establishing the new order in Aragón. Juana demonstrates how firmly empire had become a family business for the Habsburgs. Charles V, Philip's father, ruled an extraordinarily large and diverse empire, he administered Spain on behalf of his mother Juana 'the Mad,' inherited the Netherlands and Habsburg lands of Germany and Austria from his father, and was elected as Holy Roman emperor. Charles set the precedent for depending on the Habsburg women, not just as unofficial advisers but also as regents and governors. He simply could not be everywhere at once, making it necessary, for example, that his wife Isabella act as regent in Spain.

Charles' aunt Margaret of Austria (1480–1530) was extraordinarily well connected. Her father Emperor Maximilian I had sent her to France, where she was raised for eight years by the redoubtable Anne in anticipation of a match that never occurred, besides spending three years in Spain as the intended bride of the heir Juan. Initially, Margaret was a diplomatic pawn, but by the time of her third marriage she was so clearly competent that her husband Philibert of Savoy left governance to her. However, Philibert died in

1504, and when Margaret's brother Philip the Handsome of Burgundy died in 1506, Maximilian summoned his daughter to serve as regent in the duchy of Burgundy for Philip's six-year-old son Charles. Margaret held office as regent of the Netherlands until her nephew Charles reached his majority in 1515 and stripped her of power. He soon reconsidered and restored her, especially as he could spend little time in the Netherlands himself. Margaret remained as governor of the Netherlands from 1519 until her death in 1530. She was a skilled diplomat, who negotiated the League of Cambrai in 1508 and the so-called 'Ladies' Peace' of 1529.

When Margaret of Austria died, Charles V passed the task of ruling the Netherlands on to his sister Maria, another family member who was freed to serve the dynasty by widowhood. Maria was governor of the Netherlands from 1530 to 1555, and ruled even when her brother was physically present. She had the difficult task of imposing the financial burdens caused by Charles V's politics; these were exacerbated by a growing religious rift that was worsened by Charles' demands for religious conformity. As a result, Maria had to deal with a number of revolts and threats during her long governorship, which she suppressed with characteristic firmness. Probably to help her in dealing with the region's male political elite, she cultivated a mannish image. Like her contemporary Catherine de' Medici, Maria loved hunting, and rode astride (a practice still regarded as outlandish for a woman at this time). When forced to wage war, she worked sometimes through lieutenants but also took the field in person. Nonetheless, when she resigned from her office in 1555, Maria lamented that, no matter her rank, a woman was never respected as much as a man.

After Maria retired, Philip II appointed his illegitimate half-sister, Margaret of Parma, as governor-general of his increasingly disaffected northern inheritance. Margaret, whose husband the duke of Parma remained in Italy, struggled to contain popular rebellion as, at Philip's command, she imposed legislation against Protestant 'heretics' and heavy taxes, all without adequate support. Although Margaret was replaced in 1567 by the duke of Alva, Philip towards the end of his life once more turned to a Habsburg woman, his daughter Isabel Clara Eugenia. On his deathbed, Philip made her the ruler of the Netherlands and married her to Archduke Albert of Austria, who was already serving as governor-general there. The couple ruled together. After Albert's death, Philip IV cancelled Isabel's sovereign status, but she continued ruling as governor-general until her death in 1633.

The female Habsburg governorship of the Netherlands is exceptional in European history, yet in parts of Africa it was common to give

women of the ruling family administrative roles. A particularly successful example of the practice is provided by Daca, who ruled in the Lwo area of East Africa sometime in the sixteenth century. Daca's husband made her a regional governor, and she expanded into a successful state, solidifying Lwo power across a substantial region.

UNOFFICIALLY INFLUENTIAL WOMEN

Even without formal authority, royal women, especially mothers, could exercise a profound influence on government. The case of Lady Margaret Beaufort (d. 1509), mother of Henry VII of England, is well known. She worked indefatigably to win the throne for her son, and then served as his most trusted counsellor. Less familiar to Western audiences is the extraordinary power of women in the Ottoman Empire; from the mid-sixteenth to the mid-seventeenth century they had so much political influence that the period is often called 'the sultanate of women.' In particular, the mother of the sultan (the *validé sultan*) exercised direct political power, including regencies and negotiating with foreign powers. The process visibly began with the ascension of Suleiman the Magnificent in 1520. Suleiman's mother Hafsa Sultan (c.1478–1534) clearly enjoyed prestige; this is most

BELOW: **The Westminster Abbey tomb of Lady Margaret Beaufort, countess of Richmond, mother of Henry VII of England. Margaret died in 1509, a few months after her only son's death.**

evident in the large-scale public buildings she commissioned shortly after her son became sultan. Most notable is the complex known as the Sultaniye in Manisa, which included a mosque, a religious college, a hostel, primary school and soup kitchen, all manned by a 117–person strong staff.

Suleiman took the extraordinary step of marrying his favourite concubine Hurrem (1502–58), following a century in which the Ottoman rulers had only had concubines. Hurrem was unpopular due to the belief that she dominated the sultan through sorcery, which indicates how unusual and unsavoury the Turks regarded women with a political role. The correspondence between sultan and sultana suggests that their relationship was one of affectionate collaboration. For example, when Suleiman was campaigning, Hurrem sent him information about the political situation in Istanbul. She was her husband's political confidante for most of

ABOVE: A northern European follower of Titian painted this idealized portrait of Hurrem Sultan sometime in the early seventeenth century. Hurrem was known to Westerners by the name Roxelana.

his reign. Hurrem Sultan also financed the construction of large charitable institutions in Mecca, Medina, Jerusalem, Istanbul and Edirne, working to shape her own public image and that of her husband. Hurrem ensured that her own son inherited the throne, but she was never *validé sultan* because she predeceased her husband.

The first of the great Ottoman queen mothers, Nurbanu Sultan (d. 1583) was a Venetian slave concubine who exercised a deep influence over her son Murad. During Nurbanu's regency, a ceremony known as 'the procession of the *validé sultan*' originated when the *validé* received obeisance from the entire governing elite before entering the palace, where her son also gave obeisance. Her successor, the *validé* Safiye Sultan similarly dominated her son's sultanate; the extent of her political influence is apparent in the diplomatic gift of a jewelled portrait that Elizabeth I of England sent to her in 1593. The power of the Ottoman royal women throughout this golden age was all the more extraordinary because they rarely left the harem, and when they did, they were shielded from sight. Instead, they worked through eunuchs, with queen mothers in particular ruling the vast semi-governmental world of the harem.

QUEENLY POWERS IN THE EARLY MODERN ERA

The period from approximately 1620 to 1800 saw enormous challenges and possibilities for women's rule, as it did for their male counterparts. The beginning of colonialism impacted on rulers in parts of Asia and Africa, as growing encroachment raised both the spectre and the reality of foreign interference. Under such circumstances, an inspirational female leader could rise to prominence. The growing tide of absolutism tended to limit the role of female relatives of male sovereigns, although that same absolutism could work to a woman's advantage once she held the reins of power.

OPPOSITE: 'Portrait of Catherine the Great the Legislatress in the Temple Devoted to the Goddess of Justice,' painted by Dmitry Levitsky, c.1780.

RIGHT: Anne of Austria with Cardinal Jules Mazarin. Certainly a successful political team during Anne's regency, she and Mazarin may have been secretly married.

In some regions, it became more acceptable for a woman to come to the throne since it was recognized that the position was merely ceremonial; such was the case for Empress Go-Sakuramachi of Japan (1740–1813). She held the throne from 1762 to 1771, after her brother abdicated in her favour; Go-Sakuramachi in turn abdicated to make way for her nephew. When the nephew died, she became 'guardian' of the new child emperor until her own death in 1813. Such activity sounds impressive, until one recognizes that the shoguns actually controlled Japan in this period; Go-Sakuramachi played no role in governance. The Japanese shogunate (1603–1868) is an extreme example of powerless monarchs, but Europe during this period also saw the rise of popular movements that tried to limit the role of monarchy in governance, leading to the first 'constitutional' monarchies and at times erupting in violence. It is perhaps appropriate that the early modern period ended with the decapitation of a queen, Marie Antoinette of France, who was executed at the dawn of an anti-monarchic age.

WHEN KINGS COULDN'T OR WOULDN'T

A number of early modern rulers were either invalids or simply uninterested in rule, which allowed their wives to take on a dominant role in government. Such an assumption of power was not automatic, as we can see from the varying provisions made for European rulers who were mentally ill in this period. In Denmark, both Frederick V and Christian VII suffered mental illness, however, this far from opened a path to power for their English-born queens, Louisa and Caroline Matilda respectively; indeed, the latter was nearly executed for her attempts to control government. Charlotte of Mecklenburg-Strelitz, wife of George III of Great Britain, was similarly excluded from government, although she was given legal guardianship of George when his mental condition became permanent in 1811.

By contrast, Mentewab of Ethiopia (1706–73) took control of her government in 1730 as regent for her son, but simply continued ruling when Iyasu II came of age because the young man had no interest in governing. After Iyasu died, she became official regent for her infant grandson until a rival faction assassinated him and forced the dowager to retire by refusing her choice of a new king. In Mentewab's case, Ethiopia's nobles were outraged by the favour she displayed towards her own family.

The usual narrative is that women ruled when their husbands were weak, but sometimes it is difficult to see if the ruler was truly a 'weakling,' or if

LEFT: This family portrait of Charles I of England with Henrietta Maria and their eldest children gives no hint of the baleful influence the queen is supposed to have exercised over Charles.

contemporary male opinion simply attributed any reliance on a woman to male weakness or incompetence. Certainly, males of the political elite often resented queens exercising power that they thought was more properly their own. Queens could be handy scapegoats in popular opinion, and as we witnessed in chapter four, religious divisions could lead to vicious attacks on women with an unpopular religious affiliation. It is illuminating to compare popular opinion about two queens of England who played a strong role in their husbands' reigns. Henrietta Maria (1609–69), who married the hapless Charles I in 1625, played a very active role both diplomatically and in raising money and arms during the civil war that broke out in 1641. Her influence over the king had in fact been a major factor leading to Parliament's breach with the crown in the first place, as anti-Catholic hysteria fostered the notion that the French-born queen was leading her husband by the nose to Rome. By contrast, George II of Great Britain regarded Queen Caroline (1683–1737) as his 'indispensable mainstay'. He, however, was never regarded as weak and contemporaries never branded her as a meddler; but then they were both communicants of the national Church of England.

Was Philip V of Spain really a weakling who gave his wife Isabella Farnese a substantial role in government only because he was besotted with her? She was certainly Philip's principal adviser and was passionately engaged in foreign affairs, especially with regard to regaining a Spanish foothold in Italy. Isabella was a convenient scapegoat to blame when war in Italy proved to be ruinously expensive and people saw that her children were granted principalities there. That she was believed to intimidate her husband marked her as transgressive, an 'unnatural' woman, as was her effort to retain power when Philip V died suddenly in 1746 and a son by his first marriage inherited. Isabella was forced into exile.

Similarly, it is difficult to see whether the dynamic Queen Louisa Ulrica of Sweden (1720–82), sister of Frederick the Great of Prussia, domineered her husband Adolf Frederick or was his partner. Certainly, the king relied on his wife and she fought vigorously throughout his reign (1751–71) to restore power to the monarchy after much of the traditional royal prerogative had been lost to the national assembly. Besides forming a court party that engaged in heated political fights, the queen personally led an attempted coup in 1756 after vowing vengeance against a number of senators and leaders of the noble Estates of Sweden who had stripped so much power from the monarchy. She convinced soldiers to march on a meeting of the Estates, although they were ultimately persuaded to stand down and the court lost much of its prestige in the debacle. Still, Louisa Ulrica kept 'plotting' – as sources even today tend to characterize the role of a woman working to gain or hold power.

Less overt in her methods, but still regarded as an 'evil genius,' Françoise d'Aubigné (1683–1715), marquise de Maintenon, secretly married Louis XIV of France in a morganatic ceremony in 1684. Maintenon, a non-noble who had first come to the king's attention as governess of his illegitimate children, was never recognized as queen. She had the affection and ear of an absolutist king, however, and that was what mattered. Increasingly, the ageing king shared the burdens of government with his unofficial wife, and her role became ever more central as Louis descended into depression. From 1700 onwards, Madame de Maintenon carried out many of the functions of a prime minister, including the conduct of war.

A final example of a woman who held power because of her husband's real or supposed weakness is the Mughal empress Nūr Jahān (c.1577–1645), who married Emperor Jahāngír in 1611. Jahāngír was a dysfunctional alcoholic who left Nūr Jahān and her family to run the government; she governed alone after her father died and her brother left the court. All this occurred in a society in which upper-class women were completely barred from public roles. Nūr Jahān won acceptance by negotiating within the gender rules of her Muslim state. She never broke purdah (segregation of the sexes), even hunting tigers from an elephant howdah with only the barrel of her gun protruding from the curtain. In 1626, she rode into battle on an elephant litter, and gave orders through a eunuch rather than speaking directly to men. Nūr Jahān eventually accepted retirement after her husband died.

IMPEDIMENTS TO RULE

Cultural stereotypes that declared women unfit to rule continued to dog the early modern period. Sometimes, relegation of women to the background was subtle and may have seemed almost accidental. For example, in Japan, the shogun's wife was always noble, married to cement a political alliance. Usually, however, the shogun's children were born to concubines rather than to his official wife, the shogun perhaps deliberately preventing conception to set a curb on his wife's influence or that of her family. Monogamous European monarchs did not have the option of relegating their wives to childlessness, but almost all Holy Roman empresses of the seventeenth and eighteenth centuries were shunted into a subsidiary role, in which they were subjected to emotional neglect and even overt humiliation. A striking case is that of

LEFT: Nūr Jahān, shown in this painting with Jahāngír and Prince Khurram. This contemporary painting gives some sense of the opulence and ceremonial nature of the Mughal court.

Emperor Charles VI, who completely excluded his mother and wife from government in the belief that women had too many scruples and too much goodness to rule. Even when it became clear that his heir would be his eldest daughter, Maria Theresa, he gave a position on the council of state to her husband, rather than to the woman who would actually inherit the throne.

HOW DO YOU KNOW SHE'S A QUEEN?

Queens, like kings, had an important role to play in the presentation of monarchy, regardless of whether or not they held political power. They demonstrated – through their lavish clothing, jewels, ceremonial attendants and formal etiquette – that they were 'other,' separate and above the people they ruled.

In early modern Europe, queenship became more ceremonial and public than it had been in the Middle Ages. In the sixteenth century, French regent Catherine de' Medici proved especially cunning in her use of public shows to enhance her authority, for example with the Water Festival of Bayonne, a summit meeting of the French and Spanish courts in 1565. Rulers such as Henrietta Maria in England continued the practice with elaborate courtly masques, although attendance was reserved in that case to court circles. The trend towards flamboyance and flagrant consumption as markers of royalty continued throughout the seventeenth and eighteenth centuries. To give just one example, Tsar Elizabeth of Russia owned 15,000 dresses at the time of her death.

Beyond Europe, royal women were also distinguished by special clothing, hairstyles and other displays of wealth. At times, the markers of rank were more symbolic. For example, when Captain Cook reached New Zealand in 1769, he encountered the female Māori chief (rangatira) Hinematioro. Her authority was signified by the fact that she was transported on a litter and had her own bodyguards.

BELOW: Empress Elizabeth Alexeievna, wife of Tsar Alexander I of Russia, was born Princess Louise of Baden. Her name was changed on her marriage, as was her lifestyle in the opulent Russian Court. Portrait by Jean-Laurent Mosnier (1805).

Such cultural stereotypes were, of course, often fully internalized by the women concerned. Such was the case with Mary II of England after she and her husband William III usurped the throne from Mary's father James II in 1688. Mary was the legal heir to the throne rather than her cousin William, and she enjoyed popular support, unlike the Dutch William, who was regarded with suspicion as a foreigner. Nonetheless, Mary declared that as she was William's wife, God meant her to be 'in subjection to him.' At her insistence, the two were crowned jointly, with Mary deliberately taking second place, as graphically shown in the coinage of their reign in which Mary is partially hidden behind William. In this case, the queen did rule, and she did so dynamically, when her husband was away in Holland or on campaign, but she always retired from government when William was in England.

ABOVE: **A two-guinea coin showing William III and Mary II, 1694. Although Mary was the heiress, she is overshadowed on this coin as in public life by her husband, William of Orange.**

OVERCOMING OBSTACLES TO FEMALE RULE

The impediments that European and Japanese women faced were minor compared to the obstacles Hindus or Muslims had to overcome to rule. Nūr Jahān had enough difficulty ruling with power delegated from her drunkard husband; the sovereign women of Aceh in Indonesia had to deal with Islam's absolute ban on female sovereignty. Yet overcome it they did, with four sultanas succeeding each other in the period 1641–99.

The first of the sequence was Taj al-ʿAlam Safiyyat al-Din (r. 1641–75). Her father's only son had been murdered, therefore on his deathbed the sultan named his son-in-law as successor. However, the younger man died in 1641 and Taj al-ʿAlam took the throne herself, ruling for more than three decades. Her strong and moderate rule opened the door to the political elite accepting the next three ruling sultanas – as long as they remained chaste. Yet Taj al-ʿAlam still faced opposition, and her enemies brought a fatwa all the way from Mecca forbidding female rule. Taj al-ʿAlam ignored the prohibition; Mecca was very far away. Her last female successor in Aceh, Seri Ratu Kamalat Syah, fared worse, however. After ruling from 1688 to 1699, she was deposed and replaced by her own husband, who brandished the authority of the mufti of Mecca to displace her.

Three sovereign women of southern India faced the huge impediment that, by custom, they were expected to follow their husbands in death. The first, Queen Chennammaji of the Ikkeri kingdom, refused sati (being burnt on a husband's funeral pyre) when her husband was murdered in 1671 by pretending to be pregnant. She used the time she gained by this ruse to forge ties with an important court faction, winning the support of a general who named her as monarch. Chennammaji adopted a boy as her successor and eventually turned the throne over to him, but remained prominent herself until her death in 1697.

Mangammal of the Madurai state similarly evaded sati. She had influenced her husband, reportedly through her legendary beauty and charms; when he died in 1682, she claimed that only she was capable of raising her son the heir, who was still a minor. When the new raja died in 1691, Mangammal took the throne until her infant grandson grew up, although she would hold the boy on her lap when granting formal audiences to underline the temporary and conditional nature of her authority. Her story ended badly, however; when the boy reached adulthood, he deposed his grandmother; we do not know if she fled or was killed.

More successful was Queen Ahilyabai Holkar of the Maratha Empire. When Ahilyabai's husband was killed in battle in 1754, her father-in-law prevented the widow from committing sati because he wanted her support for his own rule. Her son was his heir, but after the son died in 1767, Ahilyabai ruled in her own name for nearly 30 years. She was renowned for the great care she showed her people, and was a prolific builder of Hindu temples. These three examples suggest that if a Hindu widow managed to evade the duty to immolate herself, she faced less resentment against her power than was the case in Muslim lands.

Frequently, we encounter the assumption that women, regarded as softer and more malleable than men, would fall prey to a man's influence. Such an assumption overthrew Béti of Madagascar, who inherited from her father in c.1750. Stories that she had foreign lovers led the political elite to think that European men were influencing her decisions, although there was little firm evidence to support this view. Such was the opposition she faced, as well as diplomatic problems with the French, that Béti abdicated in her brother's favour once he grew up. It was probably also the rumour rather than the reality of male influence that provided a pretext for Marie Antoinette of

BELOW: Defiant to the last in this large historical canvas painted by François Flameng in 1885, Marie Antoinette is carried in a tumbril to her execution.

France's trial and execution in 1793. She was charged not only with scheming with her Austrian family, but also with incest.

ABOVE: **A shrine dedicated to Rani Ahilya Bai of the Holkar dynasty, in Ahilya Fort, Maheshwar, India.**

INDULGING LOVERS AND FAVOURITES

At times, however, women rulers did allow male favourites or family members to dominate them, just as has always been the case with some male monarchs. Maria Anna of Austria was regent of Spain for her son Charles V from 1665 to 1676. She proved to be highly reliant on her Jesuit advisers, compounding her misstep by favouring foreigners; eventually, a noble faction forced her to resign from the regency. While Catholic clergy were unlikely to be lovers – an exception being Cardinal Mazarin, who although never ordained as a priest, may have secretly married the widowed Anne of Austria – their impact could be profound. When Maria I of Portugal suffered a mental breakdown in 1792, it was attributed to an overly severe confessor.

Lovers were the greatest danger, at least in popular opinion, and at times that fear was justified. This can be seen in the case of Queen Caroline Matilda of Denmark and Norway (1751–75). By c.1770, it was clear that Caroline's husband Christian VII was insane. Caroline was uninterested in politics, but a faction formed around her as various parties worked to influence the

Mariana of Austria (1634–96), married her own uncle, Philip IV of Spain, in 1649 – a prime example of the inbreeding that led to the physical decline of the later Habsburgs.

OPPOSITE: **The 1772 arrest of Queen Caroline Matilda of Denmark, as depicted in** *Cassell's Illustrated History of England*, **1865. Caroline Matilda was an English princess by birth.**

king. She soon started an affair with the king's physician, who became a virtual dictator thanks to his control over the king and influence over the queen. The lover was overthrown in a coup in 1772 and executed. Caroline Matilda was arrested and barely avoided execution herself; instead, she was divorced despite being mother to the heir. She died in 1775, at only 23 years old. However, Caroline Matilda's disgrace did not mean the end of women's involvement in this Scandinavian government. Christian VII's stepmother, the dowager queen Juliana Maria, stepped up and took rule.

THE STRONG MOTHERS OF THE SEVENTEENTH CENTURY

Spain, France and the Ottoman Empire all underwent extended periods under the rule of female regents, as children repeatedly inherited the throne and their mothers stepped forward to rule. One of the most successful of these regents, Mariana of Austria (1634–96), married her own uncle, Philip IV of Spain, in 1649 – a prime example of the inbreeding that led to the physical decline of the later Habsburgs. When Philip died in 1665, he left a kingdom on the brink of collapse and a three-year-old heir, Carlos II. During her 10 years of regency, Mariana guided the monarchy and the state from crisis with sound fiscal policies, and redefined Spain's position in Europe, finally bringing a period of peace rather than expensive wars. Carlos was ungrateful, and Mariana was exiled after he came of age. Nonetheless, she used her extensive connections to push forward Carlos' marriage and was reinstated in the regency in 1677 when her son's failing health made him unable to rule.

Mariana's contemporary, the regent of Savoy Maria Giovanna Battista (1675–84) was also slow to hand over the reins of power. Her son reached his legal majority at the age of 14, but the dowager remained in charge of government until after his 18th birthday.

BELOW: **Dressed in the extreme of eighteenth-century fashion, Queen Mariana of Austria looks thoroughly uncomfortable in this painting by Diego Velázquez of 1652–3.**

In France, two regencies were plagued by the consequences of the contempt and humiliation the regents had suffered in their time as consorts. Marie de' Medici (1575–1642), who married Henry IV of France in 1600, had an unhappy relationship with her husband, suffering constant slights and only being crowned as queen in 1610, the king finally recognizing that the ritual would strengthen Marie's position in France while he campaigned in the Netherlands. That reinforcement was more essential than Henry could have imagined – he was assassinated on the following day.

In her resentment at the treatment she had received from the French court, Marie as regent for the young Louis XIII dismissed her husband's counsellors and instead brought in Italians. The native French nobility naturally resented her rule, and Marie was pressured to declare Louis' majority when he was 14. Marie then suffered outright persecution, and in 1617 her chief adviser Concino Concini was assassinated. She herself was exiled to Blois and her confidante Leonora Concini was tried and executed as a witch. Marie raised a rebellion in 1619, the first of two military confrontations known as the Wars of the Mother and Son. She eventually reconciled with Louis and the king appointed his mother governor of Anjou. A new conflict soon arose, however, and Marie's army was defeated in battle. Marie herself was soon restored to the royal council, largely thanks to her ally Richelieu, for whom she had obtained a cardinal's hat. When Richelieu and Marie disagreed on policy, Louis XIII preferred to listen to the cardinal, and banished his mother yet again in 1631. She died, impoverished, in Cologne in 1642.

Less dramatically, Louis XIII denied his wife Anne of Austria sole regency when he died in 1643, but she seized control of the young Louis XIV's government and ruled with Cardinal Mazarin as her chief minister from 1643 to 1651.

The Ottomans also suffered a series of dynastic accidents that gave greater power to women in the first half of the seventeenth century: six sultans came to the throne in this period, all of them either minors or mentally incapable. Two queen mothers (*validé sultan*s) in particular were able to dominate the empire – Kösem Sultan (d. 1641) and Turhan Sultan (d. 1683). Kösem Sultan was the favourite of Ahmed I. A beautiful and shrewd woman, the sultan reportedly denied her nothing, although the Venetian ambassador noted that Kösem was careful not to raise state matters with her husband too often. Her influence was considerable over her 28 years as queen mother, during which time she served as regent for two of her sons. Kösem did so well that government leaders asked her to stay on as regent for her seven-year-old grandson after her second sultan son was deposed as mentally incompetent in 1648. Normally, a mother would have filled the position, but the new sultan's mother, Turhan, was still young. Soon, however, Turhan started asserting the rights of her position. It resulted in an active conflict between the two *validé*

BELOW: **The murder of Kösem Sultan, as depicted in an Austrian history of the Ottoman Empire (1694). Note the janissaries taking advantage of the chaos to loot the queen mother's apartment.**

*sultan*s as Kösem plotted to depose Turhan's son. Turhan was the victor in a palace coup, and had her chief black eunuch strangle the senior stateswoman. Turhan remained as effective ruler of the empire for over 30 years, until her death in 1683.

In the masculine world of the largely Muslim Ottoman Empire, these queens-regent had to use every tool possible to hold power. Like the *validé sultan*s of the sixteenth

century, they ruled for the most part through eunuchs, rarely appearing before men who were not their relatives. The vast financial resources of Ottoman queen mothers also helped; they received tax income from crown lands, their husbands or sons bestowed land grants on them and they enjoyed a daily stipend that allowed them to court public opinion with spectacular displays of piety, in particular building mosques and charitable institutions. Kösem Sultan, for example, had a mosque complex constructed in 1640 that sported an inscription over the entrance emphasizing her role. Turhan Sultan went one better with the Yeni Cami Mosque complex (1665) and two fortresses. The Ottoman queen mothers also systematically courted rising statesmen by granting the honour of marriage to one of their daughters, often repeatedly. For example, Kösem Sultan's daughter Aysha was married off six times, and Fatma seven.

SOVEREIGNTY AND WOMANHOOD

The early modern period saw a number of female rulers who controlled states in their own name. Those most easily accepted by their societies were in Africa, where many regions had long accepted shared rule with women. That acceptance eased the transition to sovereignty of the seventeenth-century Mussasa, queen of the Jaga (present-day Angola), who worked with her husband in building an empire and continued the work after he died. Mussasa led troops herself, and trained her daughter Tembandumba (who eventually succeeded her) to be a soldier. The founder of the Baulé people also found her

BECOMING A MAN

Nzinga Mbande (c.1583–1663), known as the Mother of Angola, reigned over the Ambundu kingdoms of Ndongo and Matamba from 1624 to 1663, having gained power after the death of her father and brother. Trained in her childhood as a warrior, Nzinga fought vigorously against Portuguese encroachment and led her armies in person. Oral histories tell that she was a skilled tactician.

Although her diplomatic skills were also considerable – she first appears in historical sources as an emissary to the Portuguese in 1622 – she suffered defeat and was expelled from Ndongo. However, Nzinga soon won another kingdom, Matamba, by conquest. In her second kingdom, Nzinga presented herself as a male chief, perhaps trying to legitimize her usurpation of power. She also took up polyandry in imitation of male polygyny. It should no longer surprise us that legend reported her as sexually insatiable, keeping as many as 30 slaves as sexual partners and then killing them once her lust had been satisfied.

Much more probable is the report that Nzinga 'became a man.' She dressed in the garb of a male chief and made the young men who attended her dress as women. The length of her reign suggests that she held the respect of her people, although we cannot know if it was because of or in spite of her experiment in cross-dressing.

way, although difficult, eased by cultural assumptions. Queen Pokou (c.1700–60) lived in a matrilineal society – while the Asante had male rulers, the kings needed to bear royal blood through their mothers, and queen mothers were expected to share power with their sons. When Pokou and her supporters decided to split off and form a new state after losing a succession dispute, she could count on male willingness to follow her. The oral tradition told of a harrowing journey to the new land, pursued by enemies and threatened by panthers, elephants, giant ants and snakes. They only won their way to safety when Pokou sacrificed her own son to the spirits of the flooding Comoé River – a bridge formed allowing their escape. The Baulé state came to occupy much of what is now Ivory Coast. Pokou herself did not live long after the founding of her kingdom; she was succeeded by a niece.

It was much harder for the few sovereign ranis of India to gain and keep the support of their people. As we have seen, simply surviving as widows was a challenge for Hindu royal women. Those who survived appear to have been accepted as rulers only because no male of the dynasty was available. An interesting case is Tārā Bāí, rani of Maratha, who took over the throne in 1700 when her husband was killed in battle against the Mughals. Tārā Bāí ruled for seven years, ably leading the ongoing fight against the Mughal invaders. When the Mughal threat ended, however, her late husband's nephew escaped from Mughal custody and came to claim the throne. Tārā Bāí contested what many regarded as his usurpation for years, but ultimately failed in her bid to retain the throne.

A middle path is apparent in the situation European sovereign women faced, queens who inherited their thrones and ruled in their own name. As discussed earlier, Mary II of England, although the heir, refused to rule without her husband William III and was crowned together with him. William therefore remained in place as monarch after Mary's death from smallpox at a young age; the heir of the childless couple was Mary's younger sister Anne (1702–14). England had made massive steps towards constitutional government with the Declaration of Rights (1689) to which William and Mary had agreed in return for the throne. Ulrike Eleanora of Sweden also had to accept a great reduction in royal power before the Riksdag (Swedish parliament) would offer her the throne after her brother's death in 1718. Ulrike Eleanora soon

OPPOSITE: **Hand-coloured lithograph of Nzinga Mbandi, queen of Ndongo and Matamba, imagining what she might have looked like nearly two centuries after her death.**

BELOW: **Maharani Tārā Bāí leading her troops, from a 1927 illustration.**

ABOVE: **The 2018 film *The Favourite*, directed by Yorgos Lanthimos, is a dark look at the complex relationship between Queen Anne (Olivia Colman) and Sarah Churchill (Rachel Weisz).**

abdicated in favour of her husband; Anne of England, by contrast, gave little political recognition at all to her husband, George of Denmark. George's arms were not quartered with the queen's and his name did not even appear on the coinage of her reign. George's main role was biological, fathering 17 children. Probably as a result of those multiple pregnancies – most of which ended in miscarriage or stillbirth, with only one child surviving to age 11 – by the time Anne became queen, the 37 year old was an invalid. She never attempted to challenge Parliamentary rule, although her influence in appointments – or that of her favourite, Sarah Jennings Churchill – remained very large.

The case of María of Braganza (1734–1816), who inherited the throne of Portugal on her father's death in 1777, more closely resembles that of Mary II of England. María, although the heir, drew her uncle into governance by marrying him, then ruled jointly until Pedro III died in 1786. After that, María ruled alone until her mental breakdown in 1792. What is striking about her case is that although her son was of age, he did not become king in his mother's place but instead ruled as prince regent, as was also the case with Emperor Charles V when ruling the Spanish kingdom of his mother Juana 'the Mad.' In other words, the courts of the Iberian Peninsula explicitly recognized that the heiress was ruler, rather than merely a placeholder. María never regained her sanity; when she was transported to Brazil with the rest of the royal family after Napoleon's invasion, she screamed much of the way, fearing that her own servants would torture her.

SOLE HOLY ROMAN EMPRESS

Another Maria – Maria Theresa of Austria (1717–80) – was the most successful of western Europe's female kings. Maria Theresa succeeded her father as king of Bohemia and Hungary in 1740. In the same year, she married Franz of Lorraine, who was elected Holy Roman emperor in 1745. Franz had

BELOW: This formal family portrait of Maria Theresa with Emperor Franz I and their children celebrates the empress' fruitfulness as a mother. Painting by Martin van Meytens, c.1754.

no legal rank in either Hungary or Bohemia, therefore Maria Theresa was crowned king of both. This led to an interesting predicament in the case of the Hungarian coronation, which required that the new ruler charge up a hill and brandish a sword at all four compass points; Maria Theresa had to learn to ride astride for the ceremony. This powerful queen exploited marriage to her political advantage, usually employing the title 'empress,' which she held by right because of her husband's title. Her family dynasty is still known as the House of Habsburg-Lorraine, with her own family name first. The start

of Maria Theresa's reign was darkened by the War of the Austrian Succession (1740–48), as Frederick the Great of Prussia, misogynistic and frankly expansionist, refused to accept Maria Theresa's inheritance of the Habsburg lands and invaded Silesia. The Habsburgs fought off the Prussian threat, and defeated Frederick again in 1760, thanks in part to Maria Theresa's skill in creating a web of international alliances.

Maria Theresa effectively combined masculine and female rulership traits. She bore 16 children, 11 of whom reached adulthood, and frequently

LEFT: Schönbrunn Palace, Vienna. Maria Theresa had this opulent palace constructed, and spent most of her time there after she was widowed.

A COLOURFUL CAREER

The most controversial of Europe's queens regnant in the early modern period was Christina of Sweden (r. 1632–54). Christina succeeded her father Gustavus Adolphus when she was only six years old. Interestingly, the regency council that ruled during her childhood (refusing her unstable mother a role) saw to it that Christina received the education appropriate to a male monarch, which included science and the study of philosophy, with René Descartes as her tutor. The young queen was acknowledged to be one of the most learned women in Europe.

The queen took on personal rule when she turned 18, and proved to be very successful. Indeed, Christina played an instrumental role in the Peace of Westphalia that ended the Thirty Years War. She is remembered more, however, for her sponsorship of learning in Sweden, which attracted scientists and artists from all over Europe to Stockholm, her 'Athens of the North.' She herself received the admiring nickname 'Minerva of the North' for her knowledge and scholarship.

Yet all was not well. The queen's extravagance caused public criticism, as did her refusal to marry. Those issues, however, paled by comparison to the public furore when it became known in 1654 that this queen of a staunchly Lutheran country, daughter of a Protestant hero of the Thirty Years War, had secretly converted to Roman

ABOVE: In this scene, Queen Christina is shown in philosophical discussion with René Descartes. Nils Forsberg, 1884, after an earlier painting by Pierre-Louis Dumesnil the Younger.

Catholicism. It was illegal for a Catholic to rule Sweden; Christina's own aunt had been excluded from the succession for marrying a non-Lutheran. Christina therefore simply quit, abdicated in favour of her cousin and moved to Paris. Only then did the former queen become interested in politics. She tried to regain the Swedish throne in 1660 when her cousin died, but her bid failed. Instead, her cousin's widow, Hedwig Eleonora, served as a semi-regent for her young son, who inherited the throne. Hedwig Eleonora had to share power with a regency council, although she was given two votes. More importantly, the dowager rebuilt the public image of the Swedish monarchy – refurbishing palaces and commissioning art – since Christina had stripped the royal residences bare with her abdication.

Christina spent the rest of her life scandalizing her contemporaries. Modern commentators would probably label her as transgendered and asexual. From the time of her coronation, her tutors had given her a taste for the less circumscribed world of men. She adopted male self-presentation and mimicry of male behaviour. After her abdication, the queen travelled under a male pseudonym, and usually dressed as a man. She remained a wonder of her age until her death in 1689.

presented herself as a mother figure both for her own brood and for her kingdoms. Although unpopular in Bohemia, the Hungarians loved their queen, giving her the affectionate (and very feminine) nickname *mokuska*, which means 'little squirrel.' However, besides learning to ride as a man, Maria Theresa also revived a Hungarian order of chivalry. That she presided over its first meeting as grand master raised eyebrows, but the queen explained that her coronation gave her masculine status. Nobody saw fit to protest further. In her 40-year reign, Maria Theresa presided over major bureaucratic reforms in her lands, introducing censuses and imposing greater administrative uniformity.

RUSSIA'S FEMALE CENTURY

Royal women in Russia had little power or influence before the eighteenth century; as late as the latter sixteenth century, Ivan IV 'the Terrible' ran through eight wives and consigned several to convents after he tired of them. Occasionally, a strong-willed woman could exercise power, but only as assistant to a male tsar, rather than in their own right. That was the case with Sophia of Russia (1657–1704). When her father died in 1682, Sophia's half-brother Peter (the Great) was proclaimed as tsar. However, Sophia convinced the palace guard to riot and won co-tsarship for her full brother Ivan V. Acting as regent from 1682 to 1889, Sophia started the practice for which Peter is famed – of bringing in European craftsmen. However, military defeats against the Tatars undermined Sophia's support and she was overthrown in favour of Peter, who had reached the age of 17. Like Ivan the Terrible's wives, she was forced to become a nun.

Royal women's opportunities shifted abruptly with Peter the Great's reforms, however, as did women's legal status in Russia more generally. All depended on the will of the autocrat, though; Peter eventually forced his first wife, Eudoxia, to become a nun. What truly opened the door for women's rule was the succession law of 1722, which ordained that each tsar could choose his – or her – own successor. The result was five female tsars in the eighteenth century, whose rule can hardly be distinguished from that of their male counterparts. The proliferation of women on the throne lasted until Catherine the Great's resentful heir, her 42-year-old son Paul, changed the succession law again, barring women from the throne.

The first of the female tsars, Catherine I (1684–1727), was an unlikely ruler for Russia. Catherine was the daughter of peasants from the Polish-Livonian borderlands; her background is extremely obscure. She entered royal circles as Peter the Great's mistress, bearing him at least five children before marrying him secretly in about 1707. There seems to have been real affection between the

Anna agreed to accept limitations to her autocracy, but tore up the agreement once she was in Moscow.

OPPOSITE: **The French portrait painter Louis Caravaque spent most of his career in Russia, winning important patrons including Empress Anna Ivanovna. This painting dates to the year 1730.**

couple; hundreds of extant letters they wrote to each other are full of warmth and share funny stories and details about personal matters. She was recognized as having a calming influence on her husband, and was the only person who could approach Peter when he was in a rage. She apparently often appealed to his sense of humour; Catherine reportedly won a pardon for a man by writing a petition in the name of Peter's favourite dog and then having the dog present the document tied to his collar. Peter openly married Catherine in 1712, impressed by her courage and judgement in a government emergency that year.

Although Peter the Great had issued his succession law in 1722, he did not name a successor before his death in 1725. Leading courtiers fretted over naming Peter's grandson, the child of a son by his first marriage, since the child's father had been executed for treason and they feared revenge. Catherine, by contrast, felt like a safer choice, and her supporters argued that by crowning her empress in 1724, Peter had demonstrated his intention to make his wife his heir. They won the support of the guards, and the widow Catherine became Tsar Catherine I. She ruled for two years, for the most part leaving government in the hands of Peter's chief minister, Alexander Menshikov, with whom she had long been allied.

Catherine's successor was Peter II, Peter the Great's grandson by his first marriage, but his untimely death at the age of 14 provided an opportunity for Anna Ivanovna (1693–1740), the niece of Peter the Great, who ruled for a decade from 1730. Again, Anna was the choice of the nobles, who thought her the best choice to enhance their own power. After all, Anna had royal blood in her veins and experience in government, but was also impoverished, and therefore she would be grateful. Best of all, she had no children, which meant the royal succession would be weakened. Anna agreed to accept limitations to her autocracy, but tore up the agreement once she was in Moscow. Anna, like Anne of England, gave too much power to a favourite; unlike the English ruler, the Russian autocrat disposed of much more ability to do harm.

Anna's favourite was her German lover Ernst Johann von Biron. Anna vested enormous power in Biron, to the point that he on occasions even acted in his own name rather than hers. He was brutal and corrupt; Russians remember this as a dark period in their history. When Tsar Anna died, she named her two-month-old son Ivan as heir, with Biron, the child's father, as regent. The nobles had had enough of Biron, however, and soon arrested him and made Tsar Anna's niece, Anna Leopoldovna, regent in his place. She did not last long, however, ousted – along with the infant Ivan – in a palace revolt led by Peter the Great and Catherine's daughter Elisabeth.

Tsar Elisabeth (1709–62) proved to be an effective and cherished ruler during her 20-year reign. Although she took lovers – indeed it was with a lover's help that she seized power in 1741 – the new tsar did not allow them to dominate her politically. In fact, the most significant of these, Alexis Razumovsky, known as the 'Nocturnal Emperor,' was the son of a peasant who drew the tsar's attention because of his fine singing voice; he never played a political role. Following in her father's project of Europeanizing Russia, Elisabeth was a great patron of the arts, who oversaw the development of ballet and theatre; she also opened many schools. What is perhaps most remarkable about her reign is that for 20 years capital punishment was abolished in Russia.

Continuing the see-saw of female-male rule, Elisabeth named her nephew as heir, although the German-born Peter III only lasted six months on the throne. Again, a male tsar was overthrown in a woman-led coup, this time commanded by his own wife, Catherine. Catherine II, the Great (1729–96), became by far the most famous of Russia's female tsars, ruling from 1762 until her death. A German princess who had no hereditary claim to the Russian throne, Catherine proved to be Russia's second great Westernizer, the political heir of Peter the Great.

No court in the world was as sexually permissive for women as that of Russia, and Catherine II's sexual tastes became a matter of gossip and moderate scandal. Tsar Catherine gained power in a coup, after her husband threatened to divorce her and marry his mistress, only thanks to the support of her own lover and his family. This first major lover, Grigory Orlov, was uninterested in politics. Catherine does appear to have enjoyed a period of sexual promiscuity in the 1750s, but after that her love life settled down. One of her lovers, Grigory Potemkin, was a major statesman, but Catherine never gave up her own active role in government; she may have married Potemkin secretly. After Potemkin, Catherine's lovers were on average 30 years younger than her and were politically insignificant. Her detractors, who would have found nothing unusual in a male tsar taking frequent lovers, portrayed Catherine as insatiable, even circulating stories that she enjoyed intercourse with horses, and that she died when one fell on her while being lowered with a hoist.

It cannot be doubted that Catherine the Great ruled Russia. An indefatigable worker, she signed 14,500 decrees during her

BELOW: Catherine the Great was a patron of the sculptor Marie-Anne Collot, commissioning several portrait busts from her, including this marble one carved in 1769.

reign and wrote nearly 10,000 letters. She also wrote plays and a history of Russia and even started a translation of the *Iliad* into Russian. She certainly knew how to promote her own image, and penned a series of autobiographical works that stressed her fitness to rule. In her 34-year reign, Catherine continued policies to support arts, culture and learning. She also oversaw a major territorial expansion of her state, gaining territory from wars with the Ottoman Empire and the first partition of Poland. Above all, she built Russia into a more unified empire.

By the year 1800, had ruling women, at least in Europe, reached a point of acceptance and at least relative parity with their male counterparts? Hardly. Although the early modern period saw a surprising number of female sovereigns, in addition to female regents and royal women, who were able to leverage a position of influence or power, systemic obstacles lay in the way of equality. Except in Russia, women only came to the throne if no male of the dynasty was available. Even when a woman was the only heiress, she was likely to have been taught the accomplishments 'proper' to an upper-class girl – languages, embroidery, music – rather than the training given to male heirs. Of course, throughout the world, the ruling elite was exclusively male, and therefore a female ruler remained an anomaly in an entrenched bastion of male privilege. For female rulers to escape the curse of exceptionalism, women as a whole had to be accepted as equal members of the human race with men.

ABOVE: **The high point of the reign of Catherine the Great (1762–96), by Gregorio Guglielmi, 1767. From the Collection of the State Hermitage, St. Petersburg, Russia.**

MODERN CHALLENGES FOR MONARCHIES

The period from c.1800 to the present day has witnessed an extraordinary number of women rulers, whether sovereigns, regents or consorts. They had to confront the challenges of a rapidly changing world, a world marred by colonial aggression, revolution and war. Not least of the trials the royal women of our present era have faced has been fast- (but sometimes not fast enough) changing gender expectations, which often led queens to trailblaze a path towards equality that other women could follow. Queen Victoria famously declared Elizabeth I of England to have been a good queen but a bad woman, since women are not fitted for rule. Such gender stereotypes, already beginning to fray at the edges in the early modern period, were disproven repeatedly in Victoria's own lifetime and especially in the past century.

OPPOSITE: **The coronation of Elizabeth II at Westminster Abbey on 2 June 1953. In this ancient ceremony, the monarch was anointed and crowned queen of the United Kingdom, Canada, Australia, New Zealand, South Africa, Pakistan and Ceylon.**

RIGHT: **Ranavalona III of Madagascar (1864–1917), a photo taken after she was exiled to Algiers in 1897. Ranavalona died in 1917; in 1938, her remains were returned to her native land.**

The road towards parity has certainly not been smooth, however. In 1831, the new kingdom of Belgium adopted Salic law, which banned women from its throne, and was only repealed in 1991. When the hyper-masculine German Empire was created in 1871, it too excluded women from the throne. Since then, such adamant opposition to women's rule has become rare almost to vanishing point; even Muslim Pakistan twice put Benazir Bhutto in office as prime minister. Preference for male rule itself is subsiding; as we will see, the most entrenched bastion of ruling male privilege, male-preferred primogeniture, is now giving way around the world.

NINETEENTH-CENTURY QUEENS: TO RULE OR TO REIGN?

When Queen Victoria (1819–1901) succeeded her uncle on the throne of Great Britain in 1837, the union between Britain and Hanover, in place since the time of George I, came to an end, since Hanover followed Salic law. There was no opposition to Victoria's inheritance in Britain, although there were certainly efforts to control and dominate the badly educated 18-year-old. That lack of education, along with the 1832 Reform Act that reduced the power of the ruler, added an ambiguity to Victoria's 64-year reign that she never overcame. On the one hand, the queen had to endure five assassination attempts in the early years of her reign, malcontents blaming her for the ills of

BELOW: Franz Winterhalter's 1846 portrait of Queen Victoria and her family emphasizes the gender expectations of the Victorian age. Prince Albert, positioned in front of the queen, dominates the space as paterfamilias.

Britain's rapidly industrializing society. On the other hand, Victoria repeatedly lost arguments with her prime ministers and was subservient to her husband, Albert. Although the German Albert was never crowned king – Parliament would not stand for such an elevation of a foreigner – Victoria regarded herself as his intellectual and moral inferior. She was extremely careful not to exercise royal power over him, and in 1857 awarded him the title prince consort, which gave him precedence over everyone but herself. Albert, by contrast, was eager for power, and perhaps purposely kept the queen sidelined by getting her pregnant nine times in 17 years.

Did Victoria have power, especially in the last 40 years of her reign, when after Albert's death in 1861 she lived in virtual seclusion? She certainly exercised influence, within the constraints of Britain's constitutional monarchy – influence that ranged from the popularization of Christmas trees to administrative appointments. That her influence was feared can be seen in the scandal of the elderly queen's friendship with two of her household servants, John Brown and Abdul Karim, who were thought to dominate her. Victoria's power was most direct in the control she exercised over her large family; since her children married into the monarchies of Europe, the marriage alliances created had a real effect on European diplomacy. Even Victoria's role as a figurehead, especially after a Parliamentary act of 1876 named her empress of India, should not be underestimated. Although the queen herself was an advocate of cosy 'Victorian' domesticity, the sheer fact of a woman on the throne of the world's most powerful empire helped shift attitudes about women's abilities and rule.

Other European queens of the nineteenth century ruled within the constraints of constitutional monarchy. An interesting example is María II of Portugal (1819–53), whose whole reign became emblematic of Portugal's liberal movement. Her father had declared himself emperor of an independent Brazil, hence when João VI died in 1826, the seven-year-old María was summoned across the Atlantic to take the throne. She officially reigned 1826–28, but her absolutist uncle deposed her. María then served as figurehead in the ensuing Liberal Wars, and she – along with Portugal's liberal constitution – was restored in 1834. María's reign was largely ceremonial,

ABOVE: **Queen Victoria and her controversial Scottish servant John Brown. Brown, a groom, came to dominate the royal household, shocking courtiers with his rough and domineering ways.**

especially after her husband, the German prince Ferdinand, was proclaimed as king after the birth of their first child. Like Victoria, however, María asserted influence, and also like Victoria, she bore a large brood of children, dying after the birth of the 11th in 1853. She earned the nickname 'the Good Mother' for her care both of her own children and her subjects.

María's Iberian contemporary Isabella II of Spain (1830–1904) also inherited her throne as a child, and also had her claim contested by an uncle.

'THE SOUL OF NATIONAL VIRTUE'

LEFT: The Order of Louise. This particular cross was issued to a recipient in 1813–14.

Louise of Mecklenburg-Strelitz (1776–1810), wife of the Prussian king Friedrich Wilhelm III, was a diplomat and heroic figure, although confined within a framework of female docility. She was the first queen of Prussia to win public fame in her own right, and play a prominent role both at court and in her charitable endeavours. A highly intelligent woman, Louise informed herself about political matters and increasingly became her husband's adviser. Her short life was overshadowed by the Napoleonic Wars. After Prussia suffered devastating losses against the French, Louise met personally with Napoleon in 1807 to plead favourable terms for her country, setting aside her own view that the Corsican was a monster. Although her mission failed, she was praised for her willingness to suffer humiliation for the sake of Prussia. When Louise died at the age of 34, Napoleon supposedly remarked that Friedrich Wilhelm had lost his best minister. In tribute to her role in the war and in society generally, the widower created in 1814 the Order of Louise, a female order of merit that is comparable to the Iron Cross. Members, who were always female, were limited in number to 100 and came from across all classes. Louise, who always subordinated her own opinions to her husband's interests, has enjoyed an afterlife that might well have appalled her. Conservative German women hailed her as a model of appropriate female behaviour and founded the Queen Louise League in the 1920s. Nazi propaganda also revered her as a model of womanhood.

LEFT: **Queen Isabella of Spain, clutching her suitcase and trying to catch her falling crown, is being blown out of Spain. The cartoon's caption read: 'She has throughout her life been betrayed by those who should have been most faithful to her.'**

In Isabella's case, the Infante Carlos utterly refused to accept a female ruler; the result was a succession fight known as the Carlist Wars. Partly to gain support in that struggle, Isabella's regent, her mother Maria Christina, moved Spain from absolutism to constitutional monarchy. Isabella's adult reign cannot be regarded as successful, as she alternately supported and opposed

popular sovereignty movements, besides scandalizing Spanish society with her love affairs. She was deposed in 1868 and accepted that she would never return to the throne with a formal abdication in her son's favour in 1870.

The short-lived Brazilian Empire, ruled by a branch of the Portuguese royal family, had one female ruler who proved that the monarchy's position there was far from purely symbolic. Princess Isabel (1846–1921), daughter of Emperor Pedro II, served as regent while her father made extended trips to Europe. Her bold action ended up bringing down the monarchy in this South American state. In 1888, Isabel ordered the emancipation of all slaves, clearly believing that she wielded sufficient power to impose such a reform. She was wrong. Brazil's slaveholders rose in rebellion in 1889. Pedro was forced to abdicate, and Isabel spent the rest of her life in exile in Europe.

Queen regent Emma of the Netherlands (1858–1934), probably did the best job navigating the unfamiliar waters of constitutional monarchy. Her elderly husband, William III, had antagonized politicians with his autocratic ways. When Emma became regent in 1889 during the king's final illness, and then on behalf of their 10-year-old daughter Wilhelmina, she proved more astute, learning about political issues and meeting regularly with members of the cabinet. She won considerable good will, which she used to influence issues about which she cared. Emma retired when Wilhelmina assumed personal rule, but remained active in the life of the Netherlands, winning the soubriquet 'Queen of Charity.'

AFRICAN QUEENS

It is notable that queen mothers also exercised a profound influence outside of Europe. One of the most significant was Nandi (c.1760–1827), mother of the Zulu ruler Shaka. Nandi married King Senzangakhona in c.1787, but she and her son were eventually forced into exile. When the older king died in around 1815, Shaka returned to claim the throne and launched a great expansion of Zulu territory and power. Nandi then wreaked vengeance on the people who had mistreated her, with her son's full cooperation. Nandi was the most important influence on Shaka until her death in 1827; known as 'the Great She Elephant,' she typically ruled while Shaka campaigned. When Nandi died, her son's mourning was extravagant. It was typical to kill some members of a ruler's entourage, to attend them in death; Shaka massacred 7,000. He further ordered 12,000 warriors to guard Nandi's tomb for a year, and commanded that people stop cultivating crops in mourning. The result was a famine and a coup that displaced him.

Several other nineteenth-century African queens played leadership roles, serving as regents or sharing in their husbands' duties. The first, Mantantisi, queen regent of the ba Tlokwa in southern Africa, held power c.1817–c.1824. She personally led her people's armies, and was famous for her predatory raids. Teri'itaria, consort of the chief of the Tatuti in the early nineteenth century, also had an impressive war record, so much so that she was believed to be the incarnation of a war goddess. Ileni Hagos of the Tigrayan communities (present-day Ethiopia) was less successful. When her husband

LEFT: Shaka, founder of the new Zulu nation (1816–28). Nandi, his formidable mother, enabled Shaka's rise to power.

died in c.1837, Ileni Hagos defended her son's right to rule, with herself as regent. Her rule was strong but unpopular – she imposed high taxes, and also quarrelled with other regional rulers. Ileni Hagos was overthrown in 1841, but although no longer regent, she remained influential. Her end was tragic: she was tortured and murdered by an opponent, a classic sign that Ileni Hagos had enough power to be feared and hated. Her sons avenged her, commencing a long blood feud.

In most of Africa, however, it remained nearly impossible for a woman to inherit a throne in her own right. When they did, they were circumscribed by tradition. For example, Mamochisane, queen of the Kololo (present-day Zambia) was clearly an able woman. Her father made her governor of territory he conquered, then on his deathbed in 1851, he named her heir to his whole kingdom. Mamochisane ruled briefly, but then abdicated to make way for her brother. She wished to marry and have children, and could not have done so as ruler. At almost the same time, the Itsekiri kingdom of Nigeria suffered a succession crisis. Queen Dola was half-sister to the king who died in 1848 and vigorously demanded the right to succeed him. Eventually, she attempted to hold the kingdom together by setting up an interregnum council of state, with herself at its head, but proved unsuccessful in controlling the rival clans; her influence waned rapidly.

The Lovedu people of southern Africa provide a great exception to the almost universal preference for male rule: Queen Mujaji could make rain. This ability formed the basis for female primogeniture, which has persisted among this people since 1800. Each successive woman ruler has inherited the secret medicines and objects to bring rain, thus underlining the spiritual basis for rule among the Lovedu. Belief that rulers can intercede with divine forces on behalf of their people is, of course, common in the history of monarchy; it is unclear, however, why the Lovedu determined that such a spiritual force was particularly vested in their royal women.

THE COLONIAL THREAT

One of the most important opportunities and threats that queens outside of Europe faced was European imperialism. A number of women rose or were thrust into public prominence fighting for the independence of their lands against European influence, exploitation or actual rule. One of the most striking instances of such female rule consolidated through the struggle against Europe is the Merina Empire of Madagascar. This state existed from 1810 to 1896, and four of its six rulers were women. The Sakalava state was a prelude to empire, which covered part of the island. Queen Ravahiny ruled there for 27 years after coming to power in c.1785, and oversaw a expansion

OPPOSITE: **The inauguration of Makobo Mujaji VI as Rain Queen of the Balobedu people, 11 April 2003. Makobo Mujaji was 25 years old at the time of her installation.**

of global commerce. The great queens of Madagascar – Ranavalona I (r. 1828–61), Rasoherina (r. 1863–68), Ranavalona II (r. 1868–83) and Ranavalona III (r. 1883–97) – were her political heirs.

Ranavalona I was the most controversial of these powerful women. She had married the first king of Madagascar, and when he died (perhaps poisoned by his queen), Ranavalona took the throne in her own name and sidelined their son. The first Ranavalona reversed her husband's pro-European policies, fearing the encroachment of the French into her territories. The queen forcibly halted missionary activity and expelled all missionaries in 1835, in the process suppressing a native Malagasy Christian movement. She devoted most of her energies to forging a strong centralized state, sometimes using brutal methods, including forced labour for public works such as building roads; Ranavalona is credited with halving the population of her state during her reign. She did, however, successfully maintain a large standing army, which saved her land's independence when a joint British-French force tried to depose her in 1845. Ranavalona I's successors were neither as violent in their methods nor as successful as she was. Ranavalona III was reduced to a ceremonial role after the French conquest of 1895, and forced into exile after a revolt.

By contrast, some female rulers benefitted from the support of European powers and welcomed their arrival. Nowhere is this clearer than on the island of Madagascar. While Ranavalona I and her successors opposed French influence, Binao, who became ruler of the Sakalava state on the same island, had much more reason to fear her dominant and aggressive neighbours. Therefore, when Binao became ruler, she turned to the French for support, and was a loyal ally of the Europeans in the French-Malagasy Wars that finally overthrew the Merina Empire. Binao profited from the alliance, not only seeing the subjection of an overly powerful neighbour but was also confirmed as ruler of her own territory, albeit under French protection.

While Ranavalona I opposed French influence, Binao, who became ruler of the Sakalava state on the same island, had much more reason to fear her dominant and aggressive neighbours.

Between these two extremes, Queen Teri'imaevarua III was the last ruler of Bora Bora. She reigned from 1873 to 1895 after inheriting the throne from her aunt. The French annexed the island in 1888, but Teri'imaevarua was able to hold on to power until her abdication in 1895.

Pōmare IV of Tahiti (1813–77) was another sovereign woman who stood in the way of French imperialism. In 1827, the 13-year-old Pōmare succeeded her brother; France, seeing an opportunity, declared Tahiti a protectorate in 1843 and installed their own governor. Pōmare, recognizing France's military superiority, initially attempted diplomatic protests, but talks soon deteriorated into the bloody French-Tahitian War of 1843–47. France eventually won, but to pacify the populace, they agreed to retain Pōmare on the throne, although subordinate to a French administration.

RESISTING EUROPEAN COLONIALISM

As the nineteenth century progressed, kingdom after kingdom fell prey to European colonialism. Royal women, accepted as leaders of their people, were frequently at the forefront of the struggle, fighting for survival or advantage in the massive confusion of the European onslaught. Ndaté Yalla Mbodj, who ruled the Walo Kingdom (present-day Senegal), as another eventual victim of the French. After inheriting her office from her older sister in 1847, the French soon picked a fight with the new queen over the transport of cattle through her territory. She – and her husband, who commanded the Walo army – steadfastly resisted the French invasion that followed. They were overcome and forced into exile, where Ndaté Yalla Mbodj died in 1860. Nonetheless, her staunch bravery made her a symbol of resistance to colonialism that endures to the present day.

BELOW: **Queen Pomare IV of Tahiti. Although forced to accept French administration of her kingdom, Pomare continued to fight for positions of power for her children, three of whom became rulers in their own right.**

The Akan *ahemaa* of present-day Ghana were co-rulers; the term is usually translated as 'queen mother,' which masks the institutionalized nature of their power. An *ohemaa*, the senior woman of a lineage, was not necessarily the chief's mother and was in fact inaugurated as co-ruler with a man, in what is defined as a dual male-female system of governance. These older women, the only people allowed, for example, to reprimand the king, were very powerful until British rule sidelined them.

Several of the *ahemaa* participated in the struggle against colonialism. Their people did not always listen; Afua Kobi tried and failed to keep the Asante from going to war with Britain in 1873. Yaa Akyaa, by contrast, played a more visible role. She deposed her brother, exiled him and their mother in 1884 and placed her own two sons successively on the Golden Stool of the Asante monarchy. Yaa Akyaa was fiercely anti-British and fought for her land's freedom. When the British succeeded in taking over in 1896, they exiled Yaa Akyaa along with her son and other Asante chiefs, acknowledging that she had as much power and influence as the king. Nor did that end the resistance of Asante royal women. In 1900, the Asante rebelled against British rule in a revolt instigated by Yaa Asantewaa, the *ohemaa* of an Asante sub-group, whose grandson was one of the Asante chiefs exiled in 1896. The conflict, named the Yaa Asantewaa War after her, lasted for over a year, with the queen mother personally commanding the united Asante army. She too suffered exile after her final defeat.

Several other African queens played important roles in opposition to European rule, including Lozikeyi Dlodlo, queen of the Ndebele people, in the territory that became British Rhodesia. Lozikeyi Dlodlo was King Lobengula's senior queen; the prestige of her family shored up his claim to the throne. Her family's prominence made it possible, when Lobengula disappeared, for her to assume rule herself. The queen played an important role in the military opposition to British settlement, serving as regent in 1894–96 and again from 1897 to 1909. Similarly, Gwamile Mdluli (also known as Labotsibeni) was able to move naturally into leadership thanks to the Swazi principle of dual

Djoumbe Fatima, queen of Mwali, spent her 36-year reign (1842–78) in a complex juggling act between French and Zanzibaran influence on her region.

monarchy, which installs the king and his mother jointly and expects them to rule together in everything from legal to ceremonial matters. When her husband died, the female part of the dual monarchy simply took the lead; describing her role as a 'regency' does disservice to the real situation.

Gwamile Mdluli led Swaziland – acting as the dominant partner for her young son and then her grandson throughout the period from 1899 to 1921 – worked tirelessly to reverse the sell-out of Swaziland to European interests. She was competent at regaining land that had been signed away to the British, and succeeded in preserving traditional Swazi structures. Gwamile Mdluli also introduced an extensive educational system. In her case, resistance to foreign encroachment was based on persuasion rather than military force. As spokesperson for the Swazi people, she proved to be intelligent and articulate. Others attempted war; as late as 1942, Aline Sitoe, queen of the Diola people (present-day Senegal) initiated a rebellion against French rule. The queen, still in her early twenties, was arrested and exiled, dying only two years later.

COLONIAL ALLIANCES

Not all dealings with European imperialism ended unhappily for royal women, however. Djoumbe Fatima, queen of Mwali (present-day Comoros Islands), spent her 36-year reign (1842–78) in a complex juggling act between French and Zanzibaran influence on her region. Djoumbe was in favour of alliance with Zanzibar, and married a cousin of its sultan, only to have the French expel him. Undeterred, she went on to marry two successive sultans of Zanzibar. Djoumbe Fatima eventually stood aside for her son, but was restored to the throne when the French returned in 1871.

Yoko, who inherited rule of the Kpa Meade Confederacy (present-day Sierra Leone) in 1878, was able to create a major political confederation with her neighbours, working in alliance with British colonial authorities. Among Yoko's achievements was the creation of a female initiation society, the Sande Bush, to train female leaders. Sālote Tupou III, queen regnant of Tonga, also got on well with the British protectorate under whose auspices she ruled from 1918 until 1965. Some colonial administrations even supported a woman's bid for power. Mantse Bo, who served as regent of Lesotho for 20 years (1940–60) would never have been able to establish her claim without British help. Mantse Bo was wife of a key chief of Lesotho who named his wife regent for her stepson in the event of his death. The chief's brother contested the regency, but the British high commissioner accepted it. Mantse Bo proved to be a strong ruler and a notable advocate for women's issues.

It should be noted that at times queens worked peaceably with invasive governments, however, not with independent-minded colonists. That was the fate that overtook Liliuokalani (1838–1917), who ruled Hawaii in 1891–95. The various Hawaiian islands had enjoyed many ruling queens, but Liliuokalani was the only female ruler after the kingdom of Hawaii was established in the late eighteenth century. After her brothers had ruled in succession, she became queen at the age of 53, by which time US colonists controlled the islands' economy. When Liliuokalani tried to restore some of the monarchy's power, those colonists revolted. President Grover Cleveland ordered the queen's reinstatement, but the colonists responded by setting up an independent republic. Liliuokalani's own supporters then revolted, only to go down in defeat, and the queen abdicated to win their release from American captivity.

THE RISE OF INDIA'S ROYAL WOMEN

It is impossible to discuss Western imperialism in the nineteenth and twentieth centuries without reference to India, where the British East India Company deployed its own military establishment, with the support of British regular troops, to establish a tangled web of influence, protectorate and outright rule. The whole house of cards nearly fell apart with the Indian Mutiny of 1857, a bloody fight both for independence from Britain and for the advantage of some native rulers of the subcontinent. The conflict brought several women rulers to new prominence in India, a region where not even 1 per cent of its monarchs throughout history had been women. Sometimes they sided with the British, as did Begum Nawab Sikandar of Bhopal State. She had served as regent for her daughter (1844–60), but in 1860, the British, recognizing her as a trustworthy ally, made Nawab Sikandar ruler of Bhopal in her own right, setting aside her daughter. She ruled as sovereign until her death in 1868, during which time she remained a loyal ally and instituted valuable reforms.

The regent of Oudh in northern India suffered a very different fate. Begum Hazrat Mahal, one of the concubines of the king of Oudh, was outraged when the

BELOW: Nawab Sikandar, the begum of Bhopal. This pro-British, reform-minded ruler was the first Indian monarch to perform the hajj to Mecca.

British East India Company annexed the kingdom and exiled the king. Hazrat Mahal gained support to declare her son as the new king and then helped lead the fight against the British when the mutiny broke out. After suffering defeat, the queen regent fled towards Nepal; her fate is uncertain, but she probably died of exposure along with the rest of her party.

Most famous of the women who joined and led the Indian Mutiny was Lakshmi Bai (c.1835–58), maharani of Jhansi in northern India. Lakshmi was a queen consort. When her husband fell ill, the couple adopted a five-year-old relative of his, and then when the maharaja died in 1853, Lakshmi ruled for their adopted son. The British governor-general of India refused to recognize the boy's right to the throne, however, and took the opportunity to annex

ABOVE: **The warrior maharani Lakshmi Bai. In this modern bronze statue in Solapur, this enemy of British imperialism fights as a man, all the while protectively sheltering her adopted son.**

Jhansi in 1854. Lakshmi fought the decision in the courts, only to lose. She did not have the military might to retry her case on the battlefield, and there the situation might well have ended if the mutiny had not broken out. Lakshmi was in fact recalled in 1857 to restore order after the mutiny began, only to side with the mutineers, who had provided her with an opportunity to drive the hated British from Jhansi. Lakshmi led the troops of Jhansi, reinforced by mutineers, in battle against the British, commanding them personally while dressed as a man. She was killed in battle in 1858. Lakshmi caught the imagination of her contemporaries, both Indian and British. The commander who defeated her called her the 'Indian Joan of Arc,' regarding her as the greatest and bravest of the rebel leaders.

CHINA'S MOST POWERFUL WOMAN: CIXI

Of all the women rulers who resisted foreign encroachment, the most notorious is Cixi, the dowager empress of China (1835–1908). The Qing Dynasty (1644–1911) had adhered to the Confucian principle of keeping women away from politics. Nevertheless, the force of the dynasty simply wore out; the fourth to last emperor only had three children, while the last three emperors had none. The emperors did, however, have an infusion of vigour from another source: starting in the eighteenth century they consciously preserved the Manchu identity of the imperial house by acquiring imperial consorts exclusively from Manchu hereditary military families.

Cixi came from such a family, and started her palace career as a minor concubine. She bore the emperor's only son, which gave her position when the child came to the throne in 1861. Eight male regents were appointed to rule with Cixi, but she seized power in a coup, assisted by the late emperor's principal wife, Ci'an, and several male allies. Her takeover was enabled by the role she had already played during her husband's lifetime; the emperor had lost confidence in the Taiping Rebellion (1850–64) and gradually withdrew from politics; when French and British troops occupied the capital, the emperor simply fled. Cixi, by contrast, was a strong and determined ruler at a time when nothing but confusion appeared to loom in every direction.

The dowager empress was actually regent for three distinct periods, which amounted to a total of 47 years as head of the declining Chinese state. She stepped down from her first regency when her son married, but returned to power when he died; the same was true with the successor she chose next. She retired again in 1889, but in 1898, left her retirement to lead a military coup against the emperor's '100 Days of Reform,' then served as regent for the imprisoned emperor until her death. The day before she died, Cixi ordered the poisoning of the captive emperor and named a three-year-old to the throne.

THE DEATH OF QUEEN MIN

The Korean empress-consort Myeongseong (1851–95) – known in the West simply as 'Queen Min' – played a major role in Korean politics from the 1860s. Most ruling women of Korea after the golden age of the kingdom's foundation were considered unimportant, and little is known about them. In the case of Myeongseong, however, a ruling woman became the chief locus of resistance against Japanese imperialism.

Myeongseong's husband gave in weakly to Japanese demands, accepting their virtual takeover of government. The empress, by contrast, resisted strongly and ably, and dominated Korean politics from 1874 until her death in 1895. Min proved to be a pillar

ABOVE: Colourized photograph of the funeral procession for the assassinated Korean empress Myeongseong, near Seoul, Korea, 1903. The empress' remains were taken to the royal tombs at Namyangju.

of strength against Japanese control, and even formed an alliance with Russia to resist Japan's superior power.

However, it was to be Myeongseong's determined resistance to Japan's expansionism that led directly to her assassination by Japanese agents, who broke into the royal palace. They stabbed the queen to death, then dragged her body to the courtyard, poured kerosene on it, and burnt it, to prevent even her relics from serving as a focal point for further dissent.

Observers outside the imperial circle, both Chinese and Western, found Cixi an object of fascination. Scandalmongers spread lurid tales of the dowager empress' sexual appetites, as has so often been the case when women have held power in a patriarchy. They projected stereotypical complaints about her rule, including that she interfered with the imperial succession (which was true enough) and that she had a cruel, vicious temper. Westerners believed Cixi to be implacably opposed to their interests – regarding her as inflexible and reactionary when, they felt, China would have been greatly improved by accepting European dominance.

The truth of Cixi's reign is, of course, more complex. Some accusations against her can simply be dismissed. For example, according to her own servants, the dowager was even-tempered, and she was charming to foreign guests. Indeed, modern scholarship has come around to the view that Cixi was a capable, serious monarch, who fought desperately to hold China together in the face of insuperable problems. During her long regency, China suffered repeated attacks from European powers and Cixi was forced to pay massive indemnities that further weakened a government already morally and fiscally bankrupt in the wake of the Taiping Rebellion. In her latter years, she lost considerable power to provincial governors who increasingly took an

OPPOSITE: The American artist Katherine Carl spent nine months in 1903 in China, during which she painted this portrait of Dowager Empress Cixi. Carl tells in the book she wrote about her experience that she needed the empress' special permission to look her in the face.

LEFT: French soldiers fighting the anti-colonialist Chinese rebels during the Boxer Rebellion. The Western response to the rebellion was to send 20,000 troops to China. They defeated the imperial army, summarily executed suspected rebels, and forced Cixi to agree to pay an enormous indemnity.

A FRUSTRATED EMPRESS

When Zauditu (1876–1930) became empress of Ethiopia in 1916 she had a strong female role model in her stepmother Taitu, who had been de facto ruler from 1906 to 1913 after her husband Menelik II became an invalid. Menelik had, however, resisted naming his daughter Zauditu as heir, and he was instead succeeded by a grandson. Zauditu only became empress after the grandson was deposed in 1916.

As a condition for taking the throne, Zauditu was forced to renounce her husband, and to accept her second cousin Ras Tafari Makonnen as heir. Ras Tafari gradually took more and more power, leaving Zauditu with little other than a title and some ceremonial functions. In 1928, she tried to regain control, but Ras Tafari staged a palace coup and forced Zauditu to name him as king (alongside her role as empress).

When Zauditu died in 1930, Ras Tafari was immediately crowned emperor, taking the name Haile Selassie. Clearly resentful of his long power struggle with Zauditu, Haile Selassie issued a law barring women from the throne of Ethiopia in 1955.

ABOVE: **The enthronement of Empress Zauditu of Ethiopia on 11 February 1917.**

independent line. It was probably in desperation – unable to stop them and able to see possible benefits for cooperation – that she sided with the Boxer rebels, who made a concentrated drive to end foreign influence and presence in China. The Boxers eventually failed when their massacre of Westerners resident in China brought down the military wrath of the great powers. In 1900, Cixi herself had to flee Beijing as foreign troops took the capital; she never really regained control after that. Nonetheless, her strong rule had postponed the collapse of imperial China by at least four decades.

QUEENSHIP IN AN AGE OF CONFLICT

War brings out both the best and the worst in people, and the first half of the twentieth century provided ample opportunity for royal women to prove their mettle. Both world wars in particular saw queens rally and assist troops, inspire their people and even take an active role in resistance to foreign invasion. The early decades of the century also saw the overthrow of monarchies, in particular the violent end of the Russian imperial government and the execution of the tsarina Alexandra (1872–1918), her husband Tsar Nicholas II and all their children, with Alexandra bearing much of the blame.

The judgement of history has been unkind to Alexandra, often overlooking the systemic weaknesses of the Russian Empire in favour of an explanation for the fall of the Romanovs that focuses on the deficiencies of Alexandra's personality and that of her weak-willed husband. Tsarina Alexandra certainly added to the problems of the Russian state rather than helping, however, and her ill-informed and impulsive role in politics is clear. She can perhaps be regarded as one of the sparks that finally ignited the gunpowder keg of early twentieth-century Russia.

One of the many grandchildren of Queen Victoria, the German princess married Nicholas II in 1894 and changed her name from Alix to the more acceptable Alexandra. It was a love match, opposed by Nicholas' father, which assured Alexandra's unpopularity from the start. Alexandra's own personality, introverted and publicly cold, made both the court and the population at large dislike her, a situation aggravated by her foreignness. While most royal consorts were foreigners, Germans were particularly unpopular in Russia. People were reminded of Alexandra's German blood by the fact that she spoke the court language of French poorly, and only gradually learnt some Russian.

Nicholas II did not understand the depth of crisis in his empire, and Alexandra encouraged him to behave like a traditional Russian autocrat. It was the tsarina's deep piety, normally a praised attribute of consorts, that had the most calamitous effect, however. After bearing four daughters, the couple finally produced a son, the tsarevich Alexei, in 1904. They soon learnt that the

child suffered from hemophilia, passed down from his great-grandmother Victoria. In her desperate efforts to find help for her son, Alexandra fell under the influence of the deeply corrupt faith healer Grigori Rasputin. Her reliance on Rasputin became a public scandal, while his interference in government further unbalanced the fragile monarchy.

Then came World War I, which Russia entered on the side of the Allied powers. The struggle went badly for Russia's poorly armed and equipped troops, and in 1915 Nicholas decided to go to the front personally, leaving his politically incompetent wife, suspected of German sympathies, as head of state. Alexandra certainly made a bad situation worse; she resisted political reforms and dismissed sound administrators, appointing incompetents in their place. By the time revolution broke out in March 1917, the imperial family was deeply loathed. Nicholas abdicated, and the couple along with their children, after being held in Siberia, were all shot on 17 July 1918 to prevent the possibility of their rescue and reinstatement.

Other royal women played a far more positive role in the world wars. Even as Alexandra deepened Russia's crisis, another granddaughter of Victoria, Queen Marie, was a source of great inspiration for Romania. This English-born queen consort established a network of military hospitals when war broke out in her adopted land, and personally worked in them as a nurse.

Although Romania was defeated, accepting an armistice with the Central Powers, Marie's personal appearance at the Paris Peace Conference of 1919 guaranteed favourable treatment, as she convinced the Allies to agree that Romania had fought to the last extremity. The result was an expanded Romanian state. Although Romania's period of communist rule saw an effort to blacken Marie's memory, labelling her a promiscuous drunkard, she is now once again remembered as a model of patriotism.

In the wake of World War I, a number of monarchies fell, including Germany's empire. Other European lands simply overthrew a pro-German ruler without abolishing the institution. Such was the fate of Marie-Adélaïde, grand duchess of Luxembourg (r. 1912–19). She was regarded as too supportive of Germany and bowed to pressure to abdicate. Luxembourg actually held a referendum in 1919 on whether to abolish the monarchy; 77.8 per cent of the people remained in favour of the monarchy, but with a new constitution that greatly restricted the ruler's powers. Therefore when Marie-Adélaïde's younger sister became grand duchess (r. 1919–64), her role was more symbolic than political. After Germans occupied the duchy in 1940, Charlotte fled rather than risk being used as a political puppet.

Interestingly, Luxembourg had only separated from its union with the Netherlands in 1890 when Wilhelmina became queen of the latter region, since the Luxembourg government barred female succession under Salic law. However, that did not last long, as the first independent grand duke fathered six daughters and no sons, leading him to change the rule.

Queen Wilhelmina of the Netherlands (1880–1962) played a more visibly heroic role when World War II broke out. She tried to stay with the Dutch troops after the Germans invaded, only to be taken against her will to England on a British ship.

BELOW: **The beloved Queen Marie of Romania, tending a wounded soldier in one of the military hospitals she had established. Dressed like the other nurses, most soldiers probably did not realize their queen was nursing them.**

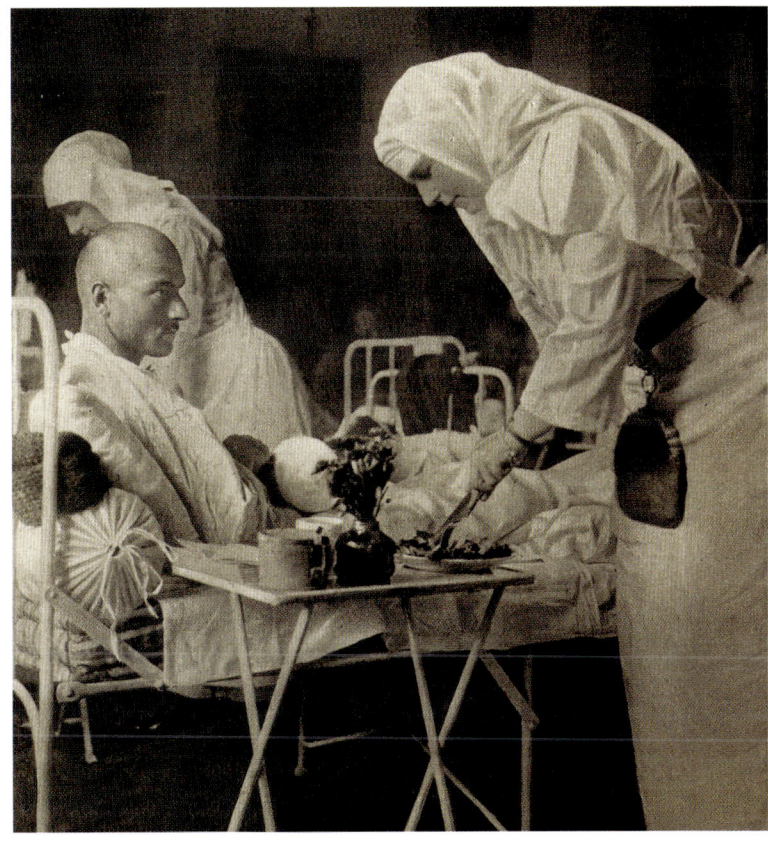

In enforced exile, Wilhelmina became an important voice of resistance in weekly radio broadcasts and on her return at the end of the war, she toured the Netherlands on a bicycle to assess the country's needs. She refused to allow heat or electricity in her own palace until infrastructure was restored in the country as a whole. Queen Elizabeth of Great Britain, the consort of King George VI, undertook a similar role in giving moral support.

Sālote Tupou III, queen regnant of Tonga from 1918 until her death in 1965, was able to perform a more direct role in World War II. The leading chiefs had not wanted a female ruler and for years urged Sālote Tupou's father to remarry and produce a son – but the second marriage only led to more daughters. Under Sālote Tupou's leadership, the islands supported the Allied cause, placing resources at the disposal of the British navy and also sending Tongan troops into battle against the Japanese in the Solomon Islands.

RULING WOMEN TODAY

The period since the end of World War II has continued to provide the world with notable female rulers, although almost everywhere their role has been limited to ceremonial and inspirational functions. At times, the demand that rulers accept limitations has led to conflict, as in Swaziland, where the queen regent Dzeliwe Shongwe in 1983 refused to recognize the supreme authority of the 15-man national council. Consequently, she was physically removed as head of state. Other queens have accepted their ceremonial position and embraced their role in preserving native traditions while advocating for human rights and social justice. A striking example of this phenomenon was the powerless but influential Queen Te Atairangikaahu of the Māori

OPPOSITE: The motherly Queen Sālote Tupou III of Tonga gives a warm greeting to Queen Elizabeth II when she arrives on a visit, 19 December 1953.

LEFT: Crown Princess Mangkubumi of Yogyakarta (right) greets the Danish Crown Princess Mary upon her arrival for a state visit on 4 December 2019. Princess Mary is an Australian by birth; she met the heir to the Danish throne in a pub and married him in 2004.

A striking sign of the times is that in 2015 the sultan of Yogyakarta named his eldest daughter, Crown Princess Mangkubumi, heir presumptive to the throne.

(1931–2006). The Māori of New Zealand have had a ceremonial ruler, without political power or a constitutional role, since 1858, and in 1966, Te Atairangikaahu succeeded, a daughter of the preceding king who was elected by the chiefs of the Waikato federation from among the members of the royal family. During her 40-year reign, the Māori queen was a strong advocate of Māori culture and sports, and also an international spokeswoman for the cause of Indigenous rights. In a similar development, Mosadi Muriel Seboko became the first female paramount chief in Botswana in 2002, elected from among the royal kindred. The focus of her outreach has been sexual rights for women and the HIV/AIDS crisis.

As women's suffrage and education have taken root in much of the world, and women of all social classes have come to play a visible public role, the last obstacles to women's rule have been fading fast. Even the Islamic world has begun to see change, with royal women starting to enjoy more public prominence. A striking sign of the times is that in 2015 the sultan of Yogyakarta, an autonomous region within Indonesia, named his eldest daughter, Crown Princess Mangkubumi, heir presumptive to the throne, rather than a male relative. Intensive debate over this move still continues.

Millennia-old cultural patterns die hard. Among the most intractable cultural stereotypes in the royal houses of the world are the assumption that women should give way to men, and that a woman ruler is second-best, a last resort if no male of the lineage is available. Should a sovereign woman be subordinate to her husband? Should a queen regnant gracefully recede into retirement when her son comes of age? And what about the daughters of royal families: should their younger or less able brothers succeed simply because they have a Y chromosome? All these issues and more have marked the period from 1950 to the present.

When Elizabeth II (b. 1926) became queen of the United Kingdom she was already married. Prince Philip, who died in 2021, at times chafed at his position. He appears to have been genuinely shocked to discover that he was, as he said, 'a bloody amoeba' – the only man in the United Kingdom who could not give his family name to his own children. The question of whether the royal family would remain the house of Windsor or change to Philip's family name of Mountbatten was repeatedly raised, including the suggestion

RIGHT: **Queen Beatrix of the Netherlands signing the Act of Abdication that relinquished the crown to her son on 30 April 2013.**

RIGHT: **Queen Beatrix of the Netherlands signing the Act of Abdication that relinquished the crown to her son on 30 April 2013.**

that giving a child its mother's family name was still a sign of illegitimacy. The family eventually reached an uneasy compromise, deciding that the descendants of Elizabeth and Philip without the 'royal highness' designation should use the name Mountbatten-Windsor. This is only one example of the awkwardness that can persist when a man assumes he is head of the household, but the woman is head of the kingdom.

For decades, there was also speculation about whether Queen Elizabeth would abdicate in favour of her adult son, as many sovereign women through history have done, either willingly or under pressure. After all, Grand Duchess Charlotte of Luxembourg turned the throne over to her son in 1964 and Queen Beatrix of the Netherlands abdicated to make way for her son in 2013. However, the queens of the Netherlands had already established a tradition of abdication, with Wilhelmina handing the throne over to her daughter Juliana in 1948 and Juliana doing the same in favour of Beatrix in 1980.

Denmark, where Margrethe II has ruled since 1972, made a stunning decision in 2009, when 85 per cent of the population voted in favour of gender-neutral royal primogeniture, in other words, that the ruler's eldest child, whether male or female, should be the heir. England followed suit with the Law of Succession in 2013. Times are certainly changing.

However, is the long, long age of monarchy itself coming to an end? The dominance of representative governments throughout much of the world has suggested to many that rulers, whether queens or kings, should be consigned to the dustbin of history. Critics point to the wealth of a number of rulers, notably the resources of a queen such as Elizabeth II, and condemn monarchs as expensive drones. Recent generations of royalty, most notably the royal women of the past eight decades, suggest that, whether male or female,

LEFT: Queen Letizia of Spain and Queen Elizabeth II of the United Kingdom pose for a group photograph before a state banquet at Buckingham Palace, 12 July 2017. Letizia became queen consort of Spain upon her husband's accession in 2014.

hereditary monarchs still have a role to play, however. Outside of and yet above the ordinary political fray, women such as Beatrix of the Netherlands, Margrethe II of Denmark or Elizabeth II of England have fulfilled a valuable diplomatic and stabilizing role in their states. While they continue to be symbols of unity and continuity, the world still has a need for them.

INDEX

Page numbers in italics refer to illustrations

PICTURE CREDITS